# HOW TO GIVE AWAY YOUR FAITH

BY PAUL E. LITTLE

INTER-VARSITY PRESS
DOWNERS GROVE
ILLINOIS 60515

11th printing,
April 1972

InterVarsity Press
is the book publishing
division of Inter-Varsity
Christian Fellowship.

A few of the Bible
quotations are from the
King James Version,
but most (unless
otherwise noted) are
from The Revised
Standard Version,
copyrighted 1946 and
1952 by the Division
of Christian Education
of the National Council
of Churches.

ISBN 0-87784-553-0

Library of Congress Catalog
Card Number: 66-20710

Cartoons by Jack Sidebotham

Printed in the United
States of America

# Contents

# Preface

Each generation has the responsibility to reach its own. It must live realistically in the present as it learns from the past and anticipates the future.

Personal conversion has been called into serious question by some of the ecclestiastical leaders of our time. Our Lord's commission stands unchanged, however, as He commands us to go into all the world and preach the gospel to every creature. And it is still evident that the gospel "is the power of God unto salvation to everyone who believes."

The primary emphasis in this book is on instruction rather than exhortation. Many want to witness but are frustrated because they don't know how.

The ideas and suggestions presented have come out of face to face interaction with Christian and non-Christian students on secular campuses and in Christian schools in the USA and abroad. Church people have responded readily to the same practical ideas.

A few of the suggestions were not originally mine. I am indebted to many for their practical help, advice, and suggestions. Significant encouragement came from the enthusiastic response to part of this material which first appeared in HIS, the magazine of

Inter-Varsity Christian Fellowship. Special appreciation is due Mrs. Elizabeth Leake, former director of Inter-Varsity Press, for her editorial advice and encouragement and to Jack Sidebotham who has done the illustrations as a labor of love.

This book is launched with the prayer that many may learn a "more excellent way" of introducing others to our Lord.

Paul E. Little
Chicago, Illinois
March, 1966

# Introduction

Fifty-seven generations ago the greatest of all Christian evangelists wrote "I am not ashamed of the Gospel of Christ for it is the power of God unto salvation."

The "explosions" of the twentieth century—knowledge, freedom, space, communication—have not made St. Paul's concern obsolete. They have only made the task of communicating the explosive dynamic of the Gospel more urgent.

Out of his years of experience as Director of Evangelism for Inter-Varsity Christian Fellowship, Paul Little gives us a refreshing, creative, and contemporary book on evangelism.

This book is authoritative. Mr. Little has not written as an armchair strategist. He is a veteran of many encounters in personal and group evangelism. We have been associated together during the Billy Graham New York Crusade, at University missions, ministers' conferences, and youth conventions. I know Paul as a man who has thought deeply, acted boldly, and spoken clearly about the Christian mission.

Though much of his work has been in the student world, what Paul Little has to say will appeal to all who are concerned about evangelism today.

This book is *Biblical*. The author knows his faith. He sounds clearly the basic notes of the Christian message to a generation wandering in theological confusion.

It is *relevant*. The author knows his world. He helps us to approach our twentieth-century neighbors, not their great-grandfathers.

It is *practical*. The author knows evangelism. He does not

make the mistake of giving us the "why" and leaving out the "how".

It is *realistic*. The author knows people. He does not deal with supermen saints or stereotype sinners, but with real Christians seeking to witness to real non-Christians.

It is *Christ-centered*. The author knows his Lord. He shows us that effective witnessing is not so much a matter of mechanics, as of a genuine, honest and overflowing relationship with our living Savior.

With excitement and thanksgiving I am honored to commend this work as a key guide to witnessing today.

Leighton Ford
Charlotte, North Carolina
January, 1966

# 1. The Essential Foundation

**S**O YOU WANT TO WITNESS! I did too, but I didn't have a clue about how to do it without stubbing my toe in the process.

How about you? Do you know how to make the good news relevant? Do you know how to communicate to people to whom the gospel seems alien? How do you talk about Jesus Christ to

—the religion major who mocks your defense of a biblical teaching with, "But this is the twentieth century, John!"?

—the junior who's promoting that "leftist" action group on campus?

—the biochemist who's only a few steps away from creating "life" in a test-tube?

—the man on the street who may be one of the 150 million casualties during the first eighteen hours of a nuclear war?

—the "who cares?" party-boy across the hall?

—that office worker who's just been replaced by a thinking machine?

—the girl down the hall who's gotten everything she's ever wanted?

—the housewife trapped in suburbia, struggling to keep up with small children, the Joneses, and a dozen civic demands?

—the international student whose brilliance is frightening and who speaks four or five languages besides English?

—the victim of divorce or a broken home who can't trust anybody?

—those nearest to you: your family, your roommate, your next door neighbor?

It's easy to quote "God so loved the world . . . ," but what do the words mean? What can you say that will make sense to these people in their everyday lives?

## Realism Is Essential

We must be realistic. Times are changing faster than ever before in history. Although Jesus Christ is the same, yesterday, today, and forever, constant change characterizes everything else in life, including you and me.

We grew up playing cowboys and Indians, cops and robbers, paper dolls, or store. When he's not glued to the TV-set, today's space-conscious child prefers the "five, four, three, two, one, zero—blast-off!" jargon of modern rocketry.

Improved communication has given us a front seat on any major event, anywhere in the world. Rapid transportation is annihilating distance and space. Telstar is here; 1200-mile-an-hour jets and 8½-hour flights from Tokyo to London are soon to come. Five years from now these very examples will be obsolete.

Revolution—people taking matters into their own hands to get the political, economic, or social changes they crave—characterizes the life of countries on every major continent. More than fifty new nations have emerged since 1945.

But while men gain new ground in their hopes to mold and conquer the universe, the future of civilization seems less and less certain. The little boy's statement, "If I live to be a man, I'll . . ." isn't so humorous any more. Many world leaders and news correspondents alike share his pessimism. When, in an end of the year summary, CBS asked Alexander Kendrick from London what he anticipated—a world of peace and love or a world of chaos—he honestly acknowledged what others hesitate to admit: "With the proliferation of nuclear weapons I don't think we're going to make it."

If we do make it, where will we go? Today's trend is more and more toward science and "scientism." This increased scientific emphasis has mushroomed in recent history. Of all the scientists who have ever lived, 90 percent are alive today. It shouldn't surprise us that many people turn to the scientist and his realms of knowledge and worship them: technology is the new world religion. But it should concern us that most of civilized mankind recognizes no other possible source of ultimate truth and no other hope of salvation.

Salvation? From what? Lostness and despair characterize our age. Modern literature, for example the titles *Nausea* and *No Exit* by Jean Paul Sartre, and most existentialist philosophy suggest the sense of meaninglessness and "caughtness" prevailing in the world today. The phenomenal popularity of recent books like *Franny and Zooey* and *Catcher in the Rye* by J. D. Salinger echoes the widespread frustration of those who, longing for a "spiritual reality," find it has eluded them. Shortly before his death, Dr. Karl Gustav Jung commented, "The central neurosis of our time is emptiness." The day of self-satisfaction and permanence, of confidence that what is built today will endure for one's children, belongs to another era.

On the university campus one sees the same quest again and again. Many students long to find some meaning for life. They know they don't have the answer, but they want desperately to lay hold of it. In a recent book, *What College Students Think,* several sociologists reported statistically that a large majority of students realize a deeply felt need for some kind of religious faith to give direction to their lives.[1]

Students, Ph.D.'s blue-collar and white-collar men, housewives, doctors, statesmen, your neighbors and mine are recognizing the vacuum in their lives, a vacuum that only Jesus Christ can fill. If we are Christians who know the answer to their need, this can be an exciting time to be alive. Or it can be a terrifying time, for people by the dozens reject the Christian answer every hour. How can we show others that the good news we proclaim is a right and relevant solution for their problems? On what grounds can you and I approach that international student, religion major, or roommate and expect to be heard—and believed?

Our non-Christian contemporaries are looking for something *real*. What we offer them must be genuine enough to withstand a careful and thorough probing. Sick of phony solutions, they're even more fed up with phony people. They aren't fooled by the pious person whose religion goes only skin-deep. Nor are they attracted by naive wishful thinkers who aren't ready to face up to life's harsh realities. In presenting the Christian answer, we must dem-

---

[1] Rose K. Goldsen and others, *What College Students Think.* (New York, D. Van Nostrand Company, Inc., 1960).

onstrate its relevance as a realistic solution in specific situations. There's only one way to do this: by being realistic about Christianity and about ourselves.

## Christianity Is Realistic

Yes, Christianity is realistic. It's not so spiritual and otherworldly that it denies the existence of matter and claims that all reality is in the mind (as many popular, idealistic philosophies from the Orient do). But while affirming material things, the Christian world view sees beyond them to spiritual things, the ultimate reality.

Our Lord dealt with the crux of this reality question when He spoke to the five thousand whom He had fed with five loaves and two fish. Tremendously impressed by the power of this miraculous feat, they wanted to draft Him as their leader. But our Lord, as He always did when people followed Him for a wrong motive, withdrew from them. Next morning the people again sought Him eagerly and finally discovered Him in Capernaum. At once they demanded, "Rabbi, when did you come here?" But Jesus answered them, "Truly, truly, I say to you, you seek me, not because you saw signs, but because you ate your fill of the loaves. Do not labor for the food which perishes, but for the food which endures to eternal life, which the Son of man will give to you; for on him has God the Father set his seal" (John 6:25-27).

Our Lord acknowledges that material food is real. Matter is real. The world of cities and streets, rocks and trees and people does exist. But He is emphasizing a spiritual reality that is of greater, of ultimate value; it transcends and outlasts the material reality. He instructs us to be realistic Christians, pursuing those things that are eternal and refusing to let the things that perish possess us. By concentrating on the matters of greatest importance, those of lesser importance fall into the proper perspective. This doesn't mean that everything "material" will fall out of the picture though.

## Christ's Example

While our Lord was in this world He used real food to feed a multitude because He knew it was famished. One of our obvious first steps in following His example is to know the condition of those around us—whether they're hungry, or tired, bored, lonely, mistreated, rejected. We must understand what and how they think, how they feel, what they aspire to do and be. What we know of others will have both individual and collective aspects, but in either case, we need some knowledge of *this* generation.

We have all met Christians whose evangelistic ministry was hampered severely because they just couldn't get their message across. They must have thought they were still living in 1925 and that their listeners were back there, too. At least that's the way they presented their message. And their hearers, of course, didn't respond. Today's audience is moved by contemporary suggestions, ones that obviously apply to this decade. They want to know how gospel truths can be relevant today.

## Realism: A Christian Responsibility

That's why we as Christians must live in today's world. We have a spiritual responsibility to be informed. How up-to-date are you on current world and national affairs? Many college students have become notorious for their "ivory-tower" disinterest in such things. On many campuses less than 10 percent subscribe to any news magazine. Keeping intelligently informed about the latest trends, developments, and crises around the globe is one way to demonstrate to our acquaintances that Christians *are* realistically aware of the affairs of this life. As our non-Christian friends realize that we aren't just walking around with our heads in the clouds, they are more apt to confide in us. On the other hand, they tend to lose confidence in all Christians when they find a few who are consistently uninformed and unconcerned.

Some of us, of course, may be so absorbed with the world at large that we ignore the individual aspect, namely specific people. Then we face the problem of the fellow who wrote:

> To love the world to me's no chore,
> My big trouble's the man next door.

We need to be in contact with the world on a man-to-man and woman-to-woman basis. Sometimes reading can enlighten us about what's going on inside people as well as around them. *Time* magazine's lengthy article on guilt and anxiety (March 31, 1961), for instance, helped many of us to sense the pressurized, competitive, rat-race effect of commuter living in a modern metropolis. Usually though, it is our own personal involvement with others as individuals that deepens our understanding of them most significantly.

As we direct our witnessing to a person whom we are learning to know and "feel for," a mere presentation of head knowledge will be transformed into heart-to-heart communication.

I will never forget one Japanese Christian, a judge, who chatted with me in the dining commons of Harvard University some time ago. Speaking as a Christian, he said, "I wish you Christians in the West could realize that we from the East, who have gone through the ravages of war, starvation, suffering, political turmoil, and the loss of loved ones, have a profound wound in our hearts." And he continued, "I know that essentially the gospel is God's message of love, and that while it has social implications, it is directed primarily to man's spiritual need for redemption; but it would mean so much if only we could *know that you know* that we have this wound in our hearts."

Millions throughout the world, in West as well as East, carry a profound wound in their hearts. Their response to us and the good news we proclaim depends a lot on whether they think we really understand and care. An old Indian proverb speaks directly to us about this: "One man should say nothing to another until he has walked in his moccasins." Admittedly, this is not always possible or advisable in actuality but, in spirit at least, we need to sit where they sit and walk where they walk. When we can convey their thoughts and feelings to them in our own words, they will begin to trust us because they know that we know, and then their willingness to consider spiritual things with us will also increase. It should not surprise us that the men whom God has greatly used throughout the centuries have not just known their Bibles well; they have known men well, too. And loving both, they have made the Word relevant to the man.

## What Do Christians Offer the World?

So far we've been looking at our world today and considering individual needs of human beings in it. We've seen how imperative it is that we know and understand something about both. But if we're going to be realistic Christians, we have to take a more careful look at the spiritual dimension, too—our own spiritual dimension. What do we have to offer? Not long ago a non-Christian went to church with a friend of mine on the West Coast. At the young people's meeting and the evening service that followed, she saw and met a variety of church members. Walking home afterwards my friend asked the obvious question, "What did you think?" She replied matter-of-factly, but perceptively, "There are some people who have it and some people who don't." As a non-Christian trying to find this intangible "it," the difference was obvious to her. Non-Christians are carefully examining the church and its individual members to see if they really have found an eternal dimension in life. A superficial profession won't convince them; they're looking for the real thing—genuine, living faith. They don't always see it though, and not because they're spiritually blind either. Sometimes it just isn't there.

## 1. Environmental Faith

The problem of mere "environmental faith" is plaguing the church of Jesus Christ today. I use this term to describe spiritual life when it's largely an outgrowth of our surroundings: Sundays we always go to Bible classes and worship services where we hear the Bible expounded. During the week we attend prayer meetings and say our little piece. Much of our time is spent with Christian friends; we speak the same language. But that's about the extent of our Christian life. We don't know what direct, personal communication between ourselves and the living God is. Some mysterious sort of osmosis is supposed to make us "spiritual." Result? When the non-Christian looks at us he sees a reflection of our environment (which he does not share) but nothing more. And it doesn't impress him. He's not looking for an environment. He's looking for living faith.

If we move out of our safety zone—by going to college for instance—we may be in for a shock. Suddenly we're faced with the shallow superficiality of our Christian experience. On secular campuses I have all too often met students whose familiar Christian environment of home and church (and perhaps school) has been stripped away. Among them, those who had never learned to live each day with Jesus Christ in a personal, vertical relationship soon found their second hand faith disintegrating. To avoid drifting unconsciously into a similar confidence in environment (faith on a horizontal basis), we frequently need to ask ourselves, "Is there anything in my life that can be explained only because of God Himself? Or is everything due to my background, surroundings, and present circumstances? What if, a week from now, my environment should be completely different?"

## 2. "Oozing into" Christianity

Besides avoiding environmental faith, we need to beware of the often-unconscious attitude that we can "ooze into" Christianity. This harmful tendency develops easily, especially in Christian homes. Recently my own little children have impressed me anew with this problem. Small Paul skips through the house singing, "I'm happy, happy, happy, happy all day long because Jesus is a friend of mine." I know he's happy most of the time, especially if he's not being punished. I also like to think that Jesus is his friend. But this verse, like so many other religious songs that we start teaching our youngsters as soon as they can talk, expresses experiential truths that my son has not yet experienced. He probably doesn't really know what he's singing—he's too young; but neither do we a lot of the time.

It has been observed, wisely I think, that hymns and choruses frequently make liars of us. We sing of glorious Christian experiences as though they were our own. But often they aren't, and so we tend more and more to accept an unreal experience as the norm. We don't realize that we're actually living a lie. Then, too, we mouth untruths musically when we sing a hymn of commitment but don't willfully make that commitment for our own lives. Unless we're careful, our rich heritage of Christian music may lead us to substitute a fiction for "the real thing."

## 3. Believing FACTS Is Not Enough

There's another substitute that some of us may have unwittingly accepted. That substitute is merely believing *facts* about Jesus Christ instead of being dynamically related to the Person who embodies these facts. I've met more than a few college students who could honestly say, "I believe everything about Christ," but they had to add, "It doesn't mean a thing to me. My faith is like Pepsi that's lost all its fizz." Why should life-as-a-Christian be like cold mashed potatoes? Why should it be insipid and burdensome as well? It shouldn't, but for some of us it is.

Have we forgotten that becoming and being a Christian involves more than some*thing* to *believe*? There is also some*one* to *receive* and to go on receiving, living with, and responding to. Giving mental assent to a list of propositions about Jesus Christ does not equal being a Christian and knowing Him personally.

Being a Christian requires continual commitment of one's self to a living Lord. This commitment depends on a relationship of love and obedience—like the relationship in marriage (the New Testament's illustration of our relationship to Christ). We smile at the bachelor who says, "Sure, I believe in marriage. I'm sold on it. You should see all the books I've read; I'm an expert on the subject. Besides, I've been to plenty of weddings. Funny thing though —can't quite understand it: marriage doesn't mean a thing to me." But while we smile, some of us may be just like him. Although we know all *about* Jesus Christ, we don't know the Lord Himself. Perhaps we've never asked the big question, never personally invited Him into our lives to be our living Lord and Savior. Or perhaps we're sometimes tempted to ask Him to be less than the Lord who demands our continual and willing obedience.

Some of our Lord's most solemn words are recorded in Matthew 7:21 where He warns His disciples, "Not everyone who says to me, 'Lord, Lord,' shall enter the kingdom of heaven, but he who does the will of my Father who is in heaven." Entering the kingdom is not a matter of using correct vocabulary or going through the proper motions; salvation is not earned by obedience. But the issue is obedience; obedience is the evidence of our life-transforming experience of new birth—birth into a life of willing commitment to Jesus as Lord. John assured his fellow Christians, "by this we may be sure that we know him, if we keep his commandments" (I John 2:3), and the whole letter of James amplifies these words.

Faith, in its very nature, demands action. Faith *is* action— never a passive attitude. For instance, if a man staggered into your room and informed you that the building would be blown up in five minutes, you might quickly show him to the door, saying that you believed him. But if you were still in the building five minutes later, he would conclude that you hadn't believed his warning. Similarly, I might claim to believe that Jesus Christ is the Savior of the world, that life's full meaning can only be known through Him, and that apart from Him all men are under the eternal condemnation of God. But if I go on along my merry way, living by a standard of self-indulgence and personal convenience, I obviously don't put much stock in these claims. I'm not believing in the biblical sense.

If we *do* believe the Christian message and we *do* know Jesus

Christ the Lord, then non-Christians will see a relevant faith and commitment in our everyday living. Throughout the Bible we can see men's faith in God revealed through their day-by-day deeds and decisions. Joseph literally gave the empty sleeve to Potiphar's wife to avoid immorality. Moses abandoned the pleasures and privileges of a son of Pharoah to identify himself with the afflicted people of God. Elijah boldly challenged the prophets of Baal to a sacrificial contest saying, "The God who answers by fire, let Him be God." Then with apparent brashness he proceeded to dump barrels of water on his sacrifices. He knew his living, powerful God would reply, and He did. Beaten and imprisoned, Paul and Silas sang hymns of praise to their God at midnight. These were not simply pious expressions, but confessions and acts of faith from the warp and woof of everyday life.

Does the claim that we know Jesus Christ make a difference in our everyday lives, day in and day out—in our use of time, money, and strength, in our system of values? What happens Monday through Saturday? How about the way we study and why we study? Does the faith we claim make a difference in our relationships with members of the opposite sex so that, refusing to overindulge or exploit, we respect the integrity of each personality and rule out any relationship that would bring pain or grief? Also, what happens when *we* experience pain, bereavement, praise, disappointment? When the chips are down, does the non-Christian see in us an attitude toward life that he'd like to have, or is he more apt to say to himself (as many *justifiably* have), "I've got enough problems of my own; don't bother me with yours!"? Finally, does knowing Jesus Christ influence our future—choosing a major, a career, a graduate school, a wife, a job?

### 4. How Do You Treat God?

Answers to questions like these help to measure the genuineness of our personal experience with Jesus Christ, but they show only part of the picture. How about God Himself? Do we really think of Him and treat Him as a living Person? Have we that heart-hunger and thirst that compel us day by day to get away—alone with Him—to study His Word and take time to talk to Him in prayer? Many of us sing about a "Sweet Hour of Prayer" and avoid it like the plague. Are we being honest with ourselves? Was it really this morning, or was it a week ago, a month ago, a year ago, or never that we last met with the Lord, just the two of us?

Non-Christians first need to detect the reality of genuine Christian experience in our lives. *Then* they will be attracted by our words about Jesus Christ and what it means to know Him personally. After I have spoken to a group, students often approach me with personal questions: "How does it work?" "How can I have the kind of life you've been talking about?" "Is there any hope for *me*?" It's always a privilege to sit down and explain how forgiveness, cleansing, and power can be individually ours in and through the Lord Jesus Christ.

## Be Honest with Yourself

Each one of us has been reading through this chapter with different attitudes, different reactions, different conclusions about himself. Some of us are convinced that our faith in the Lord Jesus Christ is genuine, but we want it to deepen and grow as our awareness of Him increases. Others of us are remembering that our faith used to seem much more relevant than it does now. Perhaps we're beginning to realize with a chill that our faith never has been any more than a mental assent to the facts about Jesus Christ and a social conformity to our Christian peers; all these years we've been concerned about the pieces of information, but not about Jesus Himself. Quite frankly, we may even be questioning whether such a thing as genuine faith or a personal relationship with Jesus Christ is possible.

Whatever our individual situations, let's at least be honest with ourselves and not put up a front to impress someone else. In the presence of God we can each ask ourselves whether we have genuine faith, faith that's actually meaningful every day. If we can answer "yes" with assurance, we ought to thank God again for His goodness and grace and ask Him to deepen and extend our faith in each experience of life. Those of us who aren't sure that our answer is "yes," or who know that we must say "no," can come to Him just as we are, simply telling Him that we want to know Him and to have faith in Him and that we are prepared to put ourselves completely in His hands.

Total and irrevocable commitment to Jesus Christ, commitment which is renewed every day, is the prerequisite for a vital relationship with the Lord. When we begin to "hold out" on Him in some area or to rebel against His will (even in some "minor" detail), our spiritual vitality suffers. A spiritual short circuit causes a snag in communications. We say we're willing to witness for the Lord on campus: "But please, Lord, don't ask me to befriend Joe; anyone but him, Lord." Or, like one young medical student, we volunteer to serve the Lord overseas, "But Lord, don't make me go to Africa. I just couldn't go there!"

How prone we are to think that we must choose *between* God's will and our own happiness, as if God wanted us to be miserable! Our heavenly Father loves us; Jesus Christ died for us; the indwelling Holy Spirit is His promise to us. Certainly this Triune God is not about to shortchange us in life. Let us come to Him as we are, whatever our circumstances, and ask the Lord Jesus Christ (for the hundredth time, or the first time) to live in us as Lord and Savior and to fill our lives with genuine Christian experience.

As we come to Him without reservation He will move in our lives, enabling us to witness faithfully to Him. When He is Lord of every part of our lives we find that He is relevant to every aspect, even when we aren't consciously aware of His presence. And as we seek to share our personally significant message of salvation with others, He will guide us into a growing awareness and understanding of them and their world (which is also ours, and His) so that His gospel will be conveyed in love and relevance— realistically—to those for whom He died.

REMEMBER: *To witness effectively we must be realistic: genuine in our knowledge of people in today's world and genuine in our total commitment to Jesus Christ.*

*Phonies or hermits need not apply.*

# 2. How To Witness

WHAT do we mean by "witnessing"? Spouting a lot of Bible verses to a non-Christian? Not quite. "Witnessing" involves all that we are and therefore do; it goes far beyond what we say at certain inspired moments. So the question is not *will* we witness (speak), but *how* will we witness? When we're trusting Jesus Christ as Lord as well as Savior, He enables us to live and speak as faithful witnesses.

Often we naively assume, however, that once we move into a vital relationship with the Lord, all our witnessing problems will disappear. In assuming this, we underestimate the problems. A genuine, personal faith in, and knowledge of, the Lord is an absolute prerequisite, for Jesus Christ is the life and substance of our Christian witness. Only He can dynamically motivate us, constraining us to share His love with others. But other factors also must be present for us to be intelligent and effective witnesses.

In talking with hundreds of Christian students across the country, I've discovered some common problems which I also had in "getting through" to another person. The difficulty usually boils down to this: when it comes to talking with someone about the gospel, we're clumsy and awkward. A lot of us just don't know how to approach people; though we've built up a head of steam, we're still preparing for that great tomorrow that's never come. We're like the enthusiastic coach, inspiring his team in the locker room, "Here we are undefeated, untied, unscored upon . . . and ready for our first game!" We've never risked spoiling our record by going out to face the opposition. And our record will continue to be a perfect blank as long as we continue to avoid the necessary contacts.

## Awkward Attempts at Witness

Perhaps some of us, under pressure from well-meaning Christian friends and numerous exhortations to witness, have made at least one awkward attempt to speak for the Lord; but we've come away feeling as unnerved as an elephant on ice! A mutually traumatic experience began as we clumsily moved in on our unsuspecting listener. Bludgeoned by our rude attack, the victim made a mental note to steer clear of us in the future (or at least run as soon as we hinted at religion). As for us, we crawled away groaning, "I don't want to see him again, ever." Then and there we retired from our short-lived ministry of personal witness and settled for a spot behind scenes. "I'll stuff envelopes and lick stamps," we volunteer. "And if you want me to, I'll even put up posters and pass out hymnbooks. But someone else can talk to people about Jesus Christ—like Bruce, he has a natural gift of gab." Most of us who know the Lord don't know how to move out into His world; instead we have withdrawn from it. So while 98 percent of us sit back and let the pros and the "gifted" do the job, the gospel continues to be little known and still less believed.

## When Christians Withdraw

By our withdrawal we deprive many of their only opportunity to hear the gospel. We also stifle ourselves spiritually, for we are denied the experience of seeing people genuinely born into the family of God. When we see no evidence of its redemptive power, the gospel begins to seem less real. If we are repeatedly hearing the claims and promises of Christ but never observing any impact, any positive response, any changed lives as a result of them, we will inevitably begin to wonder (in the secrecy of our hearts, at first, for we wouldn't dare voice this doubt): "Is the gospel really true after all? Does it have any power?" A pall of unreality may soon cover our spiritual life. Our prayers become vague; our Bible study becomes too academic—like theological canned goods on a shelf. As we turn from the outside world in upon ourselves, we may self-righteously concentrate our attention on fellow Christians, critically scrutinizing them and finding fault.

## Obedience in Evangelism

Obedience in evangelism is one of the keys to spiritual health. It is vital to all Christians, individually and collectively. Evangelism is to the Christian life what water is to Delco dry batteries: "They're fresh until delivered to you," but they're powerless until you add water. Similarly, evangelism puts sparkle into the Christian life. When we evangelize, we pray specifically, laying hold on God for victory in the spiritual struggles within the soul of an individual we care about. We ask God to illumine that one specifically, to introduce him to the Savior and a new life, to use us or any other means He may choose to get through to him. With anticipation we watch God answer prayer. We see indifference or antagonism ebb and interest grow. Meanwhile, the Bible becomes increasingly alive and relevant as we see others responding to its truth. Passages that once seemed dry and extraneous appear practical and pertinent. And remarkably, when we're concentrating on evangelism we don't have time to pick at other Christians and their faults. As we earnestly unite in proclaiming the Lord's redemptive message, we forget minor weaknesses and irritations, and the sins that worry us most are our own.

Let's review for a moment. We've agreed (1) that a genuine, personal relationship with Jesus Christ as Lord is prerequisite to being a Christian witness; (2) that Christian witness involves our whole life; (3) that involvement in evangelism is an essential vitamin for a growing experience with the Lord and a vital Christian life. But we've also admitted a basic problem: we often don't know how to witness verbally. More specifically, we don't know how to communicate the gospel graciously on a person-to-person basis.

In coping with the problem let's recognize a basic fact. Every Christian is a missionary. Any person who has been born into the family of God through faith and trust in Jesus Christ automatically receives the Lord's commission. Paul informed the Corinthians, "We are ambassadors for Christ" (II Corinthians 5:20). To guard against misunderstanding or shirking of duty, he several times restates the fact that the ministry of reconciliation has been committed to us. God makes His appeal through you and me. We stand in Christ's stead beseeching men to be reconciled to God (II Corinthians 5:18-20). What a realization, when it finally grips us! Have you ever really considered this—that you are Jesus Christ to a lot of people? Nobody else. *You* are Jesus Christ to them.

Tremendous responsibility and infinite privilege are entrusted to us as representatives of Christ. For our encouragement, Peter reminds us that the Lord guides us by His own example (I Peter 2:21). We should "follow in His steps" in all aspects of our lives, witnessing included.

## Seven Principles for Action

From our Lord's interview with the Samaritan woman at a well near Sychar, for instance, we may discover some practical, basic principles to follow as we try to represent Him in a realistic, natural way. We know of only one discussion between our Lord and this woman from Samaria (John 4). Then, as at numerous other times, He compressed all His "witness" into a single conversation. Sometimes, especially when we travel, we meet and talk with a person whom we never see again. Usually though, we have repeated contacts with a limited number of non-Christians—like our roommate, lab partner, neighbor, relative, or co-worker on the job. While we should be alert to the "one time" opportunity, it would seem that our primary witnessing responsibility is to the continuing group. Yet, somehow we clam up most when a chance comes to talk about the Lord to someone we know well. We wouldn't think of doing anything outlandish in his presence—we have to live with him—though we might risk being more decisive with the stranger whom we'll never see again.

### 1. Contact Others Socially

Now let's look at our Lord at work and pick out the main principles on which He built this single interview. Let's consider particularly how we may apply these principles in an extended relationship with a non-Christian.

Let's begin at the beginning:

*Now when the Lord knew that the Pharisees had heard that Jesus was making and baptizing more disciples than John (although Jesus himself did not baptize, but only his disciples), he left Judea and departed again to Galilee. He had to pass through Samaria. So he came to a city of Samaria, called Sychar, near the field that Jacob gave*

*to his son Joseph. Jacob's well was there, and so Jesus,
wearied as he was with his journey, sat down beside the
well. It was about the sixth hour.*

*There came a woman of Samaria to draw water.*

The first principle is obvious: we must have social contact with
non-Christians. Yet it is being ignored in many Christian circles.
This simple fact explains a lot of the apparent powerlessness of
the gospel in today's world. Both in our Christian groups (churches
and otherwise) and as individuals, we often see no one come to
Jesus Christ because no non-Christians are listening to our message. The Holy Spirit can't save saints or seats. If we don't know
any non-Christians, how can we introduce them to the Savior?

When our Lord called Simon and Andrew, He said, "Follow me
and I will make you become fishers of men" (Mark 1:17). Among
other things He was teaching that to catch fish one must go where
fish are. A simple Simon with his line in a barrel is a pathetic
figure. Yet some of us seem to be just that in evangelism. We hold
evangelistic meetings with few or no non-Christians present! The
fish avoid our barrel in droves. We must go where they are if we
are to gain any significant audience for the gospel.

At a recent all-campus lecture series, for example, several
hundred students faithfully turned out for each of the evening
lectures in the university auditorium. That was wonderful. But we
reached thirteen hundred non-Christian students by going to them
in their fraternities, sororities, and dormitories. Although very few
of these thirteen hundred students could have been persuaded to
attend the lectures, they heard us willingly and with growing interest. And a number became Christians right in their own houses!
We still value the lectures and need to use many approaches to
win others for the Kingdom. But the fact remains that we often
reach the significant numbers when we go out to meet them on
their own ground.

Let's look at our Lord's attitude again, in another incident.
The self-righteous Pharisees became very upset because He associated with sinful people. "Just look at the kind of people with
whom He's talking—and even eating!" they were saying. "Why
He's a friend of publicans and sinners!" But He answered them
(Catch that irony in His voice!), "Don't you understand? I have
not come to call the righteous, but sinners to repentance" (Luke
5:27-32).

Much of our difficulty stems from falsely equating separation and isolation. A medical analogy may help us. When the Department of Health fears an epidemic of scarlet fever it tries to isolate the germ-carriers. If everyone who has the disease is quarantined the disease won't spread. Similarly, a sure preventive against the spread of the gospel is to isolate its carriers (Christians) from everyone else. The enemy of mankind attempts to do just this by persuading us to clan together and avoid all unnecessary contact with non-Christians, lest we contaminate ourselves. By his devilish logic he has convinced many Christians. Some have informed me with evident pride that no non-Christian has ever been inside their home. Feeling very spiritual, they have boasted that they have no non-Christian friends. And then they wonder why they've never had the joy of introducing someone to the Savior!

As we re-examine the New Testament's teaching, we discover that separation from the world and isolation from the world cannot be equated. In His classic prayer for us (John 17) the Lord Jesus made this clear: "I do not pray that thou shouldst take them out of the world, but that thou shouldst keep them from the evil one" (verse 15). And having safely entrusted us to the Father for our protection, He left His followers with this command "Go ye therefore and teach all nations . . ." for ". . . ye shall be witnesses unto me . . . unto the uttermost part of the earth" (Matthew 28:19, Acts 1:8).

Our present confusion between isolation and separation is no new problem, though. We detect the same misunderstanding among the first-century Corinthians to whom Paul explained, "I wrote to you in my letter not to associate with immoral men; not at all meaning the immoral of this world, or the greedy and robbers, or idolaters, since then you would need to go out of the world. But rather I wrote to you not to associate with any one who bears the name of brother if he is guilty of . . ." (I Corinthians 5:9-11). The Christians in Corinth needed to realize, as we do, that *withdrawal from those who do not know Jesus Christ is outright disobedience to the will of the Lord.*

Instead of withdrawing, we are to go out and communicate with the world. We need to discover how, practically, we can initiate and develop friendships with non-Christians and then realistically, relevantly, and lovingly explain to them the gospel of Jesus Christ. So let's see what some of the possibilities are.

Being a Christian student on a secular campus offers unlimited opportunities. As a general rule, we might share with non-Christians more of the time and activities that we ordinarily reserve for our Christian companions (or more honestly, our Christian clique). Going shopping, attending concerts and plays, watching a ball game, eating meals, studying together, and numerous other activities can thus be redeemed for eternity.

We might also join the choral society, debating club, student newspaper, or some other campus organization that appeals to our personal interests and abilities. As we participate in campus life, we will be contributing to it positively while also having natural contacts with non-Christians.

Those of us who live near the campus or commute might invite students whom we get to know in lab or lecture hall to spend a weekend in our homes, thereby laying the ground work for a meaningful friendship.

Attending a Christian college presents a unique problem because there seem to be so few non-Christians around. With initiative and effort, though, we can develop some of the following possibilities for fruitful contact with non-Christians.

An academic club (in literature, sociology, philosophy, etc.) could invite the corresponding organization from a nearby secular campus to discuss with it some issue of mutual interest. Through this informative and stimulating exchange of views, Christians may gain accurate, first-hand insight into non-Christian thinking while the non-Christians will hear a Christian approach to some relevant issue.

An informal get-together with a secular school after an athletic event provides the opportunity to acquire social ease with non-Christians as well as to develop friendships which may later be followed up personally. Sometimes a student council exchange is also possible and valuable.

Then too, some of us work part-time, either on or off campus. We may also live off campus. How about befriending a neighbor or co-worker, getting to know and love him for the Lord Jesus Christ? Just a casual wave and smile when you pass on the street is a good start.

We mustn't forget about the international students on our own or other campuses either; most of them are all alone. Even the Christian from overseas often feels lost and bewildered by our casual fast-moving pace of living. Each friend from abroad needs companionship and understanding as he adjusts to his stay here, so that when he returns to his country he will be well-prepared (not just academically but as a person and as a Christian) to lead his people.

Our own neighborhood, for those who live at home, is often the most neglected opportunity for fruitful witness. As a primary place for evangelism, the home may become a fishing net to feed the Church. The average non-Christian will walk into our home ten times faster than he'll come to our Church.

But as the Scripture says, he who has friends must be a friend himself (Proverbs 18:24). The art of friendship has been lost by many Christians because they feel their time is being wasted when it's not invested in a specifically religious activity. To be a friend may involve listening to a neighbor's troubles or participating with him in non-religious activities that are of mutual interest socially. It means actively seeking opportunities to show love by running errands, baby-sitting, and performing any other mundane but practical service that will demonstrate the love of Christ.

Coffee klatches and other social activities are not necessarily a waste of time, even though no opportunity for a direct reference to the gospel develops at the moment. If we are committing our time to the Lord, the Holy Spirit will, in His time, give natural opportunities to speak about the Savior. Many who have first become friends in this informal way have eagerly joined in a neighborhood Bible study group. Through such Bible studies and the conversations that grow out of them, many have come to know Jesus Christ and become part of His Church.[2]

There are several things to realize in implementing these ideas. For instance, we cannot expect to impose our behavior pattern on non-Christians, even though we are their hosts. Sheer courtesy may demand that someone buy a few ash trays for the student union and that we get one for our own room (provided the fire safety regulations don't prohibit smoking!). Our thoughtless rebuke of a non-Christian on a secondary issue like this frequently leads to resentment toward all Christians, and once his self-defen-

[2]For information on available study materials, write InterVarsity Press, Box F, Downers Grove, Illinois 60515.

sive shell goes up it's harder to penetrate than a concrete wall. Showing courtesy to a smoker doesn't mean you're endorsing cigarettes! Since friendship develops in a give-and-take relationship we must also be willing to be the guests of a non-Christian friend who wants to return our invitation. The art of being a gracious guest without compromise in non-Christian society is a big subject, so we'll talk about it more in Chapter Three.

Let's repeat this first principle for witnessing—be in contact with non-Christians. We should each ask ourselves, "For whom am I praying by name every day, asking God the Holy Spirit to open his eyes, enlighten him, and bend his will until he receives Jesus Christ as Lord and Savior? Is there any one person with whom I am seeking opportunities to show the love of Christ? Am I willing to take the further initiative to communicate the gospel to him as the Spirit gives opportunity?" If we discover an absence of vital contact with non-Christians, we may simply ask God to show us one person whom He wants us to befriend, pray for, love, and eventually bring to the Savior, and He will show us that one. "Lift up your eyes and see . . . ," He says (John 4:35).

## 2. Establish a Common Interest

Then we can apply the second principle: establish a common interest as a bridge for communication. Let's look back at the passage:

> There came a woman of Samaria to draw water. Jesus said to her, "Give me a drink." For his disciples had gone away into the city to buy food.

We Christians tend to pooh-pooh anything that calls for much preliminary preparation. We like to skip the "non-essentials" and get right to the point. Preludes are a waste of time, or so we think. If I'd been our Lord, I'd probably have blurted out immediately, "Lady, do you know who I am?" Our Lord didn't approach her that way. In this incident He began by referring to something in which she was obviously interested. (She'd come to draw water.) Gradually He directed the conversation away from this known interest to a spiritual reality which she knew nothing about. Most people resent being trapped in a one-way conversation by someone who moves in and expounds his theme without even bothering to find out if the listener is interested. We resent it too. It makes us start wondering if the speaker cares about us at all or if he just wants to hear his favorite little speech again.

I wish I'd learned this lesson about communicating with people sooner. About once every six months the pressure to witness used to reach explosive heights inside me. Not knowing any better, I would suddenly lunge at someone and spout all my verses with a sort of glazed stare in my eye. I honestly didn't expect any response. As soon as my victim indicated lack of interest, I'd begin to edge away from him with a sigh of relief and the consoling thought, "All that will live godly in Christ Jesus shall suffer persecution" (II Timothy 3:12). Duty done, I'd draw back into my martyr's shell for another six months' hibernation, until the internal pressure again became intolerable and drove me out. It really shocked me when I finally realized that I, not the cross, was offending people. My inept, unwittingly rude, even stupid approach to them was responsible for their rejection of me and the gospel message.

As instruments in God's hands, we must work positively and patiently to establish mutual interests with others, beginning first where their interests lie. Later on we can profitably discuss spiritual matters together. Dale Carnegie's popular book, *How to Win Friends and Influence People,* offers many apt illustrations of human personality in action and reaction, along with some sane, common-sense suggestions for improving our relationships with people. For instance, he reminds us that the voice any person likes to hear best is his own. Everyone likes to talk, but some do more than others. Many people would give anything to find someone who would just listen to them. When we listen long enough, we not only begin to know and understand an individual; we also gain his gratitude and his willingness to listen to us, enabling us later to speak relevantly to him. In this way the Holy Spirit often draws men to us and then through us tells them about Jesus Christ so that they themselves may come to Him. This is the positive approach which Dr. Bob Smith (a checkers player) has coined "three jumps into the king's row."

Some time ago our family met a couple whose impressions of

Christianity were quite negative. As we began to get acquainted, they of course discovered our involvement in Christian work—and their jaws dropped at least seventeen feet! Immediately their guard went up. Past experience had left them a mental image of what to expect from Christians.

We quickly discovered they had two special interests: flowers and the history of our town (they've lived in it since their childhood days). Although horticulture is not my purple passion in life —far from it—I've learned a great deal about flowers in the last few years. My wife and I have also listened and learned a lot about our town. Gradually, we've established a reciprocal interest in one another. When I return from a trip they often greet me with questions: "What were you doing at the University of _____? What did you say? Were the students really interested?" As I answer I am able to share with them the power and provision of Jesus Christ for every man and his individual needs. It has thrilled us as we've watched their interest grow. (During the Billy Graham Crusade in Chicago they *asked* to go along with us to an evening service. If we had invited them, I believe they would have resented it and refused to go.)

We began with these friends where they were, concentrating on their interests. We didn't fit their stereotype of Christianity. Because we willingly shared their interests and didn't condemn them for smoking and swearing, they were not alienated and offended, but have grown responsive to us and our primary concern. By the grace of God, I believe they will soon enter His kingdom.

## 3. Arouse Interest

As we read on in John 4 we can see our Lord arousing the woman's interest and curiosity in His message through two means:

> The Samaritan woman said to him, "How is it that you, a Jew, ask a drink of me, a woman of Samaria?" For Jews have no dealings with Samaritans. Jesus answered her, "If you knew the gift of God, and who it is that is saying to you, 'Give me a drink', you would have asked him, and he would have given you living water." The woman said to him, "Sir, you have nothing to draw with, and the well is deep; where do you get that living water? Are you greater than our father Jacob, who gave us the

*well, and drank from it himself, and his sons, and his*
*cattle?" Jesus said to her, "Every one who drinks of this*
*water will thirst again, but whoever drinks of the water*
*that I shall give him will never thirst; the water that I*
*shall give him will become in him a spring of water*
*welling up to eternal life." The woman said to him, "Sir,*
*give me this water, that I may not thirst, nor come here*
*to draw."*

It is fascinating to see this woman's curiosity kindled and beginning to burn as our Lord draws her along. First, He came to her where she was. Second, He showed an interest in her concerns. Now, He is using his actions and His words to arouse a positive response to Himself and His message of truth.

At this point, the impact of His action lies merely in His speaking at all. By this simple act of talking with the woman, He demolishes social, religious, and racial-political barriers. As a man He speaks to her, a woman. As a Rabbi He speaks to her, an immoral woman. As a Jew He speaks to her, a Samaritan. Thus He startles her. While she can't quite grasp His significance, she can sense the deeper dimension in His life by His refusal to discriminate against her. He is accepting her.

In following our Lord's example, how should we try to gain people's attention and interest so that God may, through us, bring them to conviction and decision? I personally believe that parading along the sidewalk in a sandwich board which reads in large, scrawly letters, "I'm a Christian. Ask me." is not the Lord's method. He did not call us to become oddballs. As we represent Christ some people *will* think we are fools, and they will tell us so, but their opinion does not give us license to indulge in bizarre behavior. Oddballism may momentarily arouse curiosity about us, but it tends to discourage true interest in the gospel. As soon as the average onlooker who might be attracted by the Christian message sees an oddball Christian, he thinks, if that's the typical behavior of a Christian I'd better forget all about Christianity. Such a negative reaction spells defeat. We need to foster a positive interest that will prompt the individual to probe deeper and discover what Christianity actually means.

That deeper, other dimension of life—which non-Christians lack but can usually recognize—should characterize us as Christians. As we spend time with a non-Christian, our sense of real purpose in life, the values we hold, those things that really consume us and our energies will reveal themselves naturally in our everyday activities. Attitudes toward people, reactions to circumstances, that quiet peace and contentment which upholds us in the midst of all life's pressures and crises will suggest the quality of our lives. If we are no different than the people around us in these areas, we need, in the Lord's presence, to determine what is missing and then ask Him to meet our need.

If our lives are full of inconsistencies, we'd better keep our mouths shut. However, I'm not suggesting that we wait for perfection before we speak to anyone. (We'll think *how* our Lord wants us to speak in a later chapter.) Satan wants to keep us quiet. One of his deceitful methods is the attempt to convince us that we mustn't witness to anyone about Jesus Christ until we're good enough to pass for Gabriel's twin. After all, we mustn't be hypocrites. This lie that we need perfection before speaking has silenced many Christians. Actually, the personal weaknesses and failings we feel most keenly are seldom noticed by the person who doesn't know Jesus Christ. For as we go along in genuine daily fellowship with Jesus Christ, the Holy Spirit both convicts us of sin *and* adds that other dimension to our lives—even though we may not feel it there. Like Moses whose face shone so brightly, others will see this quality in our lives far more readily than we ourselves can. And their curiosity may lead them beyond what we are to inquire about the source of our life in Christ.

Jesus has called us the salt of the earth, for through our lives (as He lives in us) He causes man to thirst for Him, the living water of life. If, however, we fail to acknowledge the source of our life in Jesus Christ, we confuse them and rob God of His rightful glory. The non-Christian may merely conclude that Jane or Jim is a wonderful person and wish that he were, too. Until we bear witness to Christ, he won't have an inkling as to the source of the life he admires and wants.

Sometimes the question is asked, "Which is more important in witnessing, the life I live or the words I say?" This question throws the consistency of our lives and our verbal witness into a false antithesis. It's like asking which wing of an airplane is more important, the right or the left! Obviously both are essential and you don't have anything without both. Life and lip are inseparable in an effective witness to Christ.

Since, in reacting against high-pressure evangelism, many of us tend toward a passive silence, we need to learn how to be aggressive spokesmen for the Lord without being obnoxious. Our Lord teased the Samaritan woman into asking a question by what He said. This is a principle we may follow also. Once the non-Christian takes the first step in initiative, all pressure goes out of any conversation about Jesus Christ. It can be picked up at the point where it is left without embarrassment. On the other hand, so long as we are forcing our way against increasing resistance we tend to do far more harm than good. How can we get a non-Christian to ask a question? The answer is by throwing out bait as fishers of men and speaking to those who respond.

We cannot create spiritual interest in the life of anyone, even though we might like to. Only the Holy Spirit can do this. However, we can be instruments in His hand to uncover the interest that He has put there. We will discover so many people who are interested in spiritual reality that we won't have to force ourselves on people who are not interested. It is an enormous relief when we discover that we can legitimately drop the subject if, after throwing out the bait, we do not discover a response prompted by the Holy Spirit.

Every person I have known who has been used of God in personal evangelism has had an attitude of expectancy to discover interested people. In any group of people or in conversation with any particular individual he asks himself the question, "Lord, is this one in whom you are working?" and then, as the Spirit gives opportunity, he proceeds to see what the response is.

Relieved of the tension of forced conversation with an unwilling listener, we can talk then and later about Jesus Christ. Confident of the Lord's guidance and freed from the sense of pressure or embarrassment, we will be natural as we introduce spiritual things. In our witnessing we ought to be as relaxed and natural in our tone of voice and demeanor as we are when we're discussing last night's game, our physics assignment, a small boy's exploits, or the stock market.

But how do we throw out bait? Our Lord did it by making a cryptic statement precipitating a question from the Samaritan woman. His statement related to her primary needs and at the same time suggested His ability and willingness to meet those needs.

*Jesus answered her, "If you knew the gift of God, and*

*who it is that is saying to you, 'Give me a drink,' you
would have asked him, and he would have given you
living water." The woman said to him, "Sir, you have
nothing to draw with, and the well is deep; where do you
get that living water? Are you greater than our father
Jacob . . .?"*

We might make a statement or first ask a leading question ourselves. Jesus also anticipated the woman's reactions. Her questions did not catch Him off guard even once. To take full advantage
of each opportunity, we also need to consider the likely responses.
As we think about possible situations, let's think through how to
throw out the bait and how to handle the likely response.

After even a vague reference to "religion" in a conversation,
many Christians have used this practical series of questions to draw
out latent spiritual interest: First, "By the way, are you interested
in spiritual things?" Many will say, "Yes." But even if the person
says, "No," we can ask a second question, "What do you think a
a real Christian is?" Wanting to hear *his* opinion invariably pleases
a person. From his response we'll also gain a more accurate, first-
hand—if perhaps shocking—understanding of his thinking as a non-
Christian; and because we have listened to him he'll be much more
ready to listen to us. Answers to this question usually revolve
around some external action—going to church, reading the Bible,
praying, tithing, being baptized. After such an answer we can agree
that a real Christian usually *does* these things, but then point out
that that's not what a real Christian *is*. A real Christian is one
who is personally related to Jesus Christ as a living Person. If the
non-Christian continues to indicate interest as we explain this, we
can go on to the third question, "Would you like to become a real
Christian now?" An amazing number of people today are drifting
in a spiritual fog, yearning for someone to lead them into spiritual
certainty.

If we are talking to a friend of Roman Catholic background,
we might remark, "You know, I have a lot more in common with
you than I do with my liberal Protestant friends." He may be surprised by this comment but it will gratify him. We can then explain, "You believe in the Bible as the Word of God, in the Deity
of Christ, in the necessity of His death as an atonement for our
sins, and in His resurrection from the dead; but many liberal
Protestants deny these basic facts of New Testament Christianity."
We can then go on to say, "I suppose that in the Catholic Church

you've discovered the same thing that I see in the Protestant Church: Some Methodists, Baptists, Presbyterians, Episcopalians, etc., really know Jesus Christ personally, and some don't." Invariably he will agree and thus recognize a major fact, namely that church membership in any church does not, in itself, guarantee a personal relationship with Jesus Christ. We can then discuss with him what it means to be personally related to the Lord.

If we're on the ball, we can seize many other opportunities to throw out a leading comment. But we frequently lose out in the "art of repartee" by thinking of the appropriate comment an hour later! So let's plan ahead now for those common remarks in everyday conversation that can easily be spoken for the Lord.

Another means of throwing out the bait is to be alert for opportunities to share our spiritual experience. As we get to know non-Christians on a personal basis, they will begin to confide in us about their burdens, longings, aspirations, frustrations, and emptiness. As they tell us these things, we can say quietly (if our experience was similar), "You know, I used to feel like that until I had an experience that completely changed my outlook on life. Would you like me to tell you about it?" By making a cryptic statement and offering rather than forcing our experience on him, we prevent the other person from feeling that we're just unloading unsolicited goods at his doorstep. If he asks to hear about our experience, we should be ready to speak briefly, emphasizing the reality of Christ to us today and eliminating boring and probably irrelevant details. We should simply say what Christ means to us now, and how He has changed us.

If our experience has not been parallel to the one described to us by our non-Christian friend, but Christ is a reality to us today, we can say, "You know, I *would* feel that way except for an experience that changed my outlook on life. Would you like me to tell you about it?" Those of us who have grown up in a Christian home and church often develop an inferiority complex because we can't point to a dramatic change in our lives when we became Christians. We can't say, "Once I was a dope addict, but see what Christ has done for me!" If we came to new life in Christ as a child, we probably did not notice much change in our lives. We need not feel inferior or apologetic about this, as though somehow our experience were not as genuine as the more spectacular. Paul's conversion was wonderfully dramatic, but we must always remember that Timothy's was just as real. From early childhood he heard the Word of God from his grandmother, Lois, and his mother, Eunice. The great question is whether Jesus Christ is a dynamic reality to us today.

The bait can also be thrown out succinctly if we are prepared for questions we are asked frequently. Often we recognize after it is too late that we have had a wonderful opportunity to speak up but we missed it because we didn't know what to say at the moment. Sometimes we are asked questions like: "Why are you so happy?" "What makes you tick?" "You seem to have a different motivation. You're not like me and most people. Why?" "Why is it you seem to have purpose in life?" Again, we can say, "An experience I had changed my outlook on life." And then, as we are asked, we can share that experience of Christ with them.

Again, we are often asked a question relating to our church or some activity that can be directly related to spiritual things if we handle it properly. A question I'm often asked in traveling is, "What kind of work do you do?" I used to reply matter-of-factly, "I'm a staff member for the Inter-Varsity Christian Fellowship." Usually there would be an awkward pause and my friend would nervously shift to another subject and try over again. But then someone suggested to me that answers describing activity or function always tell more than a mouthful of proper names and titles. So now I explain my work instead: "I talk to students about how Jesus Christ relates to everyday life." The curious questioner often replies, "That sounds interesting." "It is," I say. "Just the other night I was talking to a student who said . . ." and I briefly give the gist of an actual conversation. Then I ask, "By the way, are you interested in spiritual things?" and another fruitful discussion usually develops.

In a discussion about the day's headlines, the latest world crisis, or some other current event, the query, "What do you think is wrong with the world?" may be appropriate. After listening while various external causes are blamed for mankind's problems, we can ask, "Have you ever considered what Jesus Christ said about this?" and then refer to His diagnosis of man in Mark 7:21-23. Man himself, because of his inner attitudes, is the basic problem. As G. K. Chesterton aptly put it, "What is wrong with the world? I'm wrong with the world." And the only solution to the

"I" problem is Jesus Christ, who has promised to change us as we commit ourselves to Him.

Books and booklets on provocative subjects provide another possibility for stimulating conversation on spiritual matters. Among the books for browsing in our living room—which include *Rise and Fall of the Third Reich, The Making of the President,* and *This Hallowed Ground*—we've scattered *The Christian's Secret of a Happy Life, Woman to Woman, The Evidence for God in an Expanding Universe,* and Elizabeth Elliot's beautiful pictorial book, *The Savage My Kinsman.* Guests sometimes leaf through these books and occasionally borrow one of them. Other times we may offer a small evangelistic booklet—perhaps *Is Christianity Credible?, Have You Considered Him?,* or *Becoming a Christian*— to some friend with the comment, "I'd be interested in your reaction to this. Since I don't have too many copies I'd appreciate your returning it." Having thus put a clear and concise statement about the Christian faith in his hands, we can anticipate a fruitful discussion with him about Jesus Christ before long.

In these and similar situations, knowing what we are going to say beforehand will help overcome nervousness and put us at ease. If we clutch, the other person clutches; but if we relax, he relaxes. As we gain in quiet confidence that the Holy Spirit will lead us to interested people, we can overcome any tendency to be apologetic about our faith. When we assume lack of interest by someone we tend to defeat ourselves before we start. On the other hand, if we assume interest we will usually get an interested response. Each successful encounter with a non-Christian will lead us to greater faith and confidence for the next one.

### 4. Don't Go Too Far

The next part of our Lord's conversation reveals principles four and five: give a person only as much of the message as he is ready for, and don't condemn him.

> *"Every one who drinks of this water will thirst again, but whoever drinks of the water that I shall give him will never thirst; the water that I shall give him will become in him a spring of water welling up to eternal life." The woman said to him, "Sir, give me this water, that I may not thirst, nor come here to draw." Jesus said to her, "Go, call your husband, and come*

*here." The woman answered him, "I have no husband."*
*Jesus said to her, "You are right in saying, 'I have no*
*husband'; for you have had five husbands, and he whom*
*you now have is not your husband; this you said truly."*
*The woman said to him, "Sir, I perceive that you are a*
*prophet."*

Despite her obvious interest and curiosity, Jesus didn't give her the whole story at once. Gradually, as she was ready for more, He revealed more about Himself. Then, when her curiosity had reached fever pitch (verse twenty-six) He identified Himself as the Christ.

The moment we detect a faint glimmer of interest in a non-Christian many of us want to rush right in and rattle off the whole gospel without coming up for air or waiting to sense audience response. (After all, we might not get another chance, we think!) But by relying on the power and presence of the Holy Spirit, we can gain poise. The non-Christian needs gentle coaxing when he's just beginning to show his interest: it's usually fragile at first. Otherwise, like a bird scared from a close-up perch by too rapid movement toward him, he will withdraw before our overly eager approach. On the other hand, if we are casual in our attitude and relaxed in our manner, the inquirer will tend to press us all the harder to get at the source of our quiet assurance.

## 5. Don't Condemn

In the fifth principle we see that our Lord did not condemn the woman. As she answered Him about her husband, her sin itself condemned her. In the similar incident with the woman taken in adultery whom the self-righteous Pharisees brought to our Lord, Jesus said "Neither do I condemn you; go, and do not sin again" (John 8:11). Most of us, on the other hand, are quick to condemn. Often we have the mistaken idea that if we do not condemn a certain attitude or deed, we will be condoning it. But this was not our Lord's opinion.

Unwittingly we condemn the non-Christian who offers us a cigarette, invites us to join him for a drink, or suggests some other activity that we consider out of bounds. Our reply may have devastating effects. It is almost reflex action sometimes to say, "No thank you, I don't smoke, drink, etc. I'm a Christian." Mentally we chalk up another point on our testimony scoreboard. What we've actually accomplished is this: we've condemned the person and garbled the gospel with the false implication that this particular "don't" is an inherent part of Christianity.

Thousands of non-Christians within our culture do not do these particular things; but that doesn't make them Christians. And the fact is that in some cultures some Christians do drink beer, ale, or wine, or smoke tobacco, and think nothing of it. They are none the less Christians. In both situations, custom and personal conviction determine habits. However, if a friend suggested, "Let's go rob a bank," and we said, "No thanks, I'm a Christian," he would clearly understand the connection. The eighth commandment clearly forbids stealing; there is no other way for the Christian to interpret "Thou shalt not steal."

How, then, should we answer the non-Christian whose personal customs and convictions differ from ours? The key is to recognize the compliment and generosity implicit in his offer or invitation and to decline on a personal basis so the person doesn't feel condemned or rejected. One way to say "No thanks" on a personal basis is to suggest an alternative activity. When invited to go out for a beer we might answer, "No thanks, but I'll have a coke with you sometime." Or if asked to go somewhere we'd rather not go we could respond, "Thanks, I'm not interested in that, but let me know when you're going to a concert (game, club meeting, etc.) and I'll go with you." By your suggesting an alternative the person realizes you're not rejecting him.

In declining an offer, we don't need to apologize. After all, plenty of non-Christians don't drink, smoke, dance, chew or do certain other things. If a non-Christian isn't interested in playing chess he doesn't blush, hem and haw, and finally mumble apologetically, "No thanks, I don't play chess. I'm a non-Christian." Of course not. He replies breezily, "No thanks, chess leaves me cold. But let me know when you want to play ping pong." As witnesses of Jesus Christ we can and should say "No thanks" in this same easy unembarrassed spirit.

When we find liquor being served at a function (and those of us who mix with our neighbors and associates will sooner or later), we can politely request ginger ale or fruit juice instead. If the host hasn't provided a substitute for non-drinkers, that's his social *faux pas,* not ours.

When we invite a person who smokes to our room in the dorm or our home, we must have the courtesy to provide an ash tray to put him at ease. We don't thereby endorse smoking, but we keep our non-Christian friend from being put off on a secondary issue. The only other alternatives are to force him to tap the ashes onto the rug or into his hand, or to inform him that smoking's not allowed within our hallowed walls. In either case he's likely to be offended and won't want to come back.

Not only must we avoid condemning people, we need to learn the art of legitimate compliment. Many people are deeply touched by a genuine compliment. Criticism is far more natural to our lips and to the lips of the world than praise, but praise can bring a warmth of feeling essential to an open reception of the gospel.

In *Taking Men Alive* Charles Trumbull asserts that we can discover in any person at least one thing as a basis for honest compliment. To prove his point he describes one of his own experiences on a train. A drunken man spewing profanity and filth staggered into his car. After lurching into the seat beside Mr. Trumbull, he offered him a swallow from his flask. Mr. Trumbull inwardly recoiled from the foul-mouthed inebriate. But instead of blasting the man about his condition he replied, "No thank you, but I can see you are a very generous man." The man's eyes lit up despite his drunken stupor, and the two men began to talk. That day the drunken man heard about One who has the water of life and has promised that anyone who drinks of it will never thirst again. He was deeply touched and later he came to the Savior.

## 6. Stick with the Main Issue

As the interview between our Lord and the Samaritan woman draws to a close, we note two final principles that apply to our witnessing conversations:

> *"Our fathers worshiped on this mountain; and you say that in Jerusalem is the place where men ought to worship." Jesus said to her, "Woman, believe me, the hour is coming when neither on this mountain nor in Jerusalem will you worship the Father . . . But the hour is coming, and now is, when the true worshipers will worship the Father in spirit and truth, for such the Father seeks to worship him. God is spirit, and those who worship him must worship in spirit and truth." The woman said to him, "I know that Messiah is coming (he who is*

*called Christ); when he comes, he will show us all things." Jesus said to her, "I who speak to you am He."*

Our Lord did not allow any secondary questions to sidetrack Him from the main issue. The woman asked where she should worship, on Mount Gerizim or in Jerusalem, but Jesus steered the discussion back to Himself by shifting the emphasis from where to how one worships. Though hers was probably a legitimate question (her attitude was similar to the current honest question that many people have, "Which church should I join?"), our Lord refused to go off on a tangent; He left no doubt about the main issue: Himself.

## 7. Confront Him Directly

And finally, in declaring that He was the Messiah, our Lord reached the crucial point of the gospel. Likewise, whether we spend one or many sessions building a bridge of friendship between us, we must eventually cross this bridge and bring the non-Christian into a direct confrontation with the Lord Jesus so that he realizes his personal responsibility to decide *for or against*—Him.

The people to whom we witness will fall into one of two categories initially. The first group includes those who lack the necessary information about Jesus Christ. Even if they wanted to, they wouldn't know how to become Christians. With such a person we should be alert, first, to discover the misunderstandings and gaps in their knowledge, and second, to seize each opportunity to explain more of the necessary facts.

Those in the second group are already informed about the gospel, but they haven't acted on their information yet. Our repeated thumping of the same strings and continued cramming of the same information down their throats is more apt to alienate than to win them. When we know that an individual is fully informed about the gospel, we should keep quiet, pray earnestly and daily for him by name, and love him into the kingdom of God.

These, then, are our seven principles—see and know non-Christians personally; establish a mutual interest in conversation; arouse a person's interest by life and word; gear explanations to his receptiveness and readiness for more; accept and even compliment rather than condemn; stay on the track; and persevere to the destination. Once we begin to grasp these principles and move out in faith, life becomes a daily fascination. We watch with anticipation to see the next opportunities God will give us to bear witness as ambassadors of Jesus Christ and to discover how He is working in the lives of others, through us.

*More flies are caught with honey than vinegar.*

# 3. Hurdling Social Barriers

**A**NYONE who moves out of his safety zone and gets involved in the real world is sure to run into ticklish situations. We need to consider beforehand how we may cope with some of them, working out principles that apply in varying circumstances.

## Use the Casual Touch

How, for instance, should we react to profanity or filth? Probably a lot of us tend to swish Victorian skirts around us, perhaps displaying a holier-than-thou attitude by scathing remarks or icy silence. When we react like this to non-Christians who are only doing what to them, comes naturally, we lose many potential friendships.

If we grow huffy whenever a person swears, he'll start dredging up every profane expression he's heard in the last two years and rediscover it in our hearing, just to get our goat. We've intensified the problem we were trying to solve. On the other hand, some casual humor can do wonders for a situation like this. After Harry has unwound his long string of profanity, we may comment half-jokingly but so he knows we're dead serious, "Say, Harry, your vocabulary's sort of limited isn't it?" We don't have to condemn him outright to get the point across. Once he realizes that we don't appreciate this part of his speech, he may even make a positive effort to modify his vocabulary. As we are gaining his respect instead of provoking his animosity, the problem can gradually solve itself.

## Have a Good Joke Ready

We can react to off-color stories in a similar way. If possible, of course, it's best to be absent when they are known to be the subject of conversation. But sometimes we're caught and can't excuse ourselves. Then our best course is positive preparation. Be alert for the first lull in conversation and then jump in with a good clean story. Tell one so funny that people can't help laughing. Some people think I'm joking when I say this, but I'm not. I'm convinced that every Christian should always have five sure-fire jokes at his disposal. Well chosen, well-timed humor can reset the whole tone of a conversation; it can carry you over a seemingly impossible hurdle. Like remembering names, the only way to remember a joke is to use it immediately after you hear it. If necessary, write it down afterwards. Then tell it whenever you get a chance.

A foul-mouthed person doesn't need to be told that he's groveling in the garbage pit of life. He knows he is. But he doesn't think he could enjoy life without his garbage pit. He probably thinks that Christians have to give up their sense of humor when they become Christians. He may have stereotyped the Christian as someone who can't have any fun. Our first job is to correct his negative impression of Christianity. We want him to realize that we still have our sense of humor—even though we don't indulge in his kind of fun—and that Christian enjoyments are on a higher, more lasting plane than his.

By the grace of God we can, without compromising ourselves or condoning his words, respond with love to the one who swears or tells off-color stories. It will take more than a hollow protest about our happiness in the Lord or a big front about what a ball the Christian life is. If we are natural and spontaneous in everyday situations, many of which have an amusing aspect, we can show our friend genuine, wholesome humor and the delight that we enjoy in fellowship with Jesus Christ. If we are prepared to overlook his words and demonstrate that we love him despite them, we can gain a friend.

## Begin Now—Where You Are

Right now someone's probably thinking, "Boy, this sounds good, but I would need to start over, go some place where no one knows me, then I could make a go of it. But the mess I've made—I can't redeem this situation! Who can unscramble an egg?" If you feel this way, take heart. No situation has to be a lost cause. On your part, things can be transformed.

I know a secretary who resolved before God to make a new beginning right where she was. She'd been working in the same office for eight and a half years. And every noon hour while the rest of the office staff ate lunch together, she had gone off by herself to eat and to read her Bible. She didn't want to be defiled by the world of her co-workers' repulsive language and jokes. Finally, though, she began to realize that aloofness could never promote opportunities to witness about Jesus Christ. Motivated by love for the office staff, she abandoned her aloofness and began to mix with them. Six months after her first weak-kneed but joke-supplied attempt, she joyfully told me that her office had received her openly. In those six months she had had more opportunities to share the good news with them than in all the previous years. You see, if we launch out in faith with a new loving attitude, we can make a new start where we are, no matter how bad the situation has been.

## Giving Thanks in Public

Another secondary issue that warrants some thought is the propriety of saying grace before a meal. When we're alone in a restaurant, we shouldn't have any question about bowing our head to give thanks. But as considerate Christians, what should we do when we're out with someone who doesn't know us well? When the awkward moment arrives our natural reaction is to want to conceal our action; we don't want our companion to realize what we're doing. We fumble with our napkin or clear our throat, and hope for two seconds of silence so we can pray and start eating before the meal gets cold. The waitress if she's looking must wonder if we have a headache, want to smell the food, or just happen to have a peculiar habit. Giving thanks can be embarrassing! One of my Christian friends brought me up short the day we dined together. "Shall we scratch our eyebrows?" he asked casually and caught me with my hand in mid-air. We had a good laugh, but I learned my lesson too. Before then I'd never realized how enslaved I was to this diversionary tactic.

Sometimes, unintentionally, our way of saying grace offends the other person. Our behavior implies, "You're a pagan." To avoid creating this barrier, which could deter our friend from considering the claims of Jesus Christ, it may be best for us to keep our eyes open while we thank God for our food. No verse of Scripture dictates, "Thou shalt say grace with thine eyes closed." Since thanksgiving is the purpose of saying grace, our motivation matters more than whether our eyes are opened or closed. Why am I unwilling to bow my head and give thanks? If I'm ashamed of acknowledging Jesus Christ, I need to become willing in my heart to kneel down publicly on my knees and give thanks. But if I'm truly thankful, but don't want to erect an artificial barrier between my friend and the Lord, that's another matter. Each of us knows his own motives before God. Some of us probably think of saying grace as a golden opportunity to witness by our example. It may be that —but there are dangers in this approach, especially if it will offend a dining mate.

Saying grace is still in vogue, though, like religion in general. In restaurants we often see little cards that list three prayers—for Protestants, Catholics, and Jews. My bowed head won't tell a person much about Jesus Christ. Even if he concludes that I'm religious, he won't learn anything about my Lord. When it comes to effectiveness in witnessing, saying grace can be as *un*helpful as our stating, "I don't do such-and-such because I'm a Christian."

With all these difficulties, how should we thank God for our food? In a restaurant it's best to casually say to our companion, "It's my custom to give thanks for my food. Would you like me to say grace for both of us?" Including him in the invitation implies our assumption that he says grace; he'll appreciate this implication. By our invitation we also convey the fact that we know and speak to the living God. Later we may be able to specifically ask our friend about his relationship to Jesus Christ.

The situation is a bit different in a home. In our own homes there's no question about what to do. A simple word of explanation like, "It's our custom to give thanks for our food before we eat, so John is going to say grace now," will prepare the guest. If our guest isn't a religious person, and we don't explain our custom, he may be unnerved by his uncertainty about our ritual; it's only courteous to tell him what we're about to do. The same principle applies if we have Bible reading and prayer after dinner. We don't need to apologize for our custom or alter it because we have a guest. But considering his sense of strangeness, we should keep him informed about what's happening. When, on the other hand, we are the guest and our host doesn't say grace, it would be impolite to put him on the spot by ostentatiously returning thanks ourselves. His resentment of our rudeness in this minor issue might block a later discussion of more basic issues.

## Give Specific Invitations

A broader aspect of our social involvement with non-Christians is the whole question of inviting them into our homes. We often think, "I don't have anything in common with a non-Christian;" then we're stymied. If we share no interests at all, why get together and have a flop? We're afraid he'll be bored if he joins us in some activity we like; and we dread being embarrassed if we go somewhere with him. This dilemma is easily solved by planning what we'll do together beforehand. Instead of just saying, "Joe, can you come over Tuesday evening?" or "I'm having several of the students home for the weekend. Can you come?" we can specifically suggest, "to play ping pong?" or "to go skiing?" This solves the "What shall we do?" problem at the outset. The person who's being invited knows what to expect; if he's not interested he can decline the invitation without embarrassing anyone. But nine times out of ten, he'll want to come.

We also need to think about secondary issues that arise in our relationships with a group. Many of our group associations are by necessity rather than preference. Since we don't choose the other members of the group, they seldom consider our individual behavior as a personal affront to them. Individual feelings aren't hurt as easily in a group as they are in a personal relationship. In the group, therefore, we can do things that on a personal basis we would hesitate to do for fear of condemning the friend.

## Don't Necessarily Follow the Crowd

Going to college throws many of us into group life with non-Christians twenty-four hours a day. Most fellows can also anticipate a stint with Uncle Sam. Before we enter any group situation, but especially one of considerable duration, it's good to determine exactly what habits we're going to keep as Christians, and then keep them from the beginning. If you usually give thanks for your food, remember to say grace at the first meal. If you have a daily

quiet time, include it in your schedule the very first day. If you
don't establish your pattern at the outset, each day you put it off
will make it harder to begin.

Groups often decide to do something together as a body. As
Christians, what should we do if we don't have the liberty to
participate in a proposed activity? We're members of a democratic
group that has reached a majority decision. But if we go along
with the gang we'll be unfaithful to our Lord. Whenever this is our
dilemma, whether the issue is inherent in Christianity or less directly related, we need to bow out graciously. We can explain to
our companions without beating around the bush, "I won't try to
legislate for you, but personally I can't go along with that; you'd
better count me out." Although most people today are floating
downstream, they respect the few who are fighting against the
current. In private conversations they'll admit their admiration;
they wish they had enough courage and conviction to take a stand
too. So they respect us because we're inner-directed instead of
other-directed. They will also respect us if, while we have the
courage of our convictions, we don't arbitrarily legislate for them.

## Express Love

In all of these secondary issues, a little advance thought now
can prevent much embarrassment. We aren't devising gimmicks to
get at people with the gospel surreptiously. We're seeking ways of
expressing the love of Jesus Christ. Because the Lord has come
into our lives our capacity to love is deepening. His love is being
shed abroad in our hearts to be poured out for others. We love
people for themselves, as total men rather than abstractions. If
Jesus Christ is a personal reality to us, His love will reach out
through us to some very unlovely people whom everyone else
despises; He gives us the capacity to love them as people.

As one expression of our love for them, we want to communicate the gospel. But no friendship should depend on how the
other person responds to the gospel. Unfortunately, many non-
Christians today are suspicious of all Christians because of a
previous contact with a friendly religious person who had ulterior
motives. Some non-Christians refuse to listen to a single word
about our Lord until they're sure we'll be their friends regardless
—even if they reject Jesus Christ. We must love each person for
himself.

None of us can play God for another person. We can't determine the stage of the Holy Spirit's work in his life. It may take several years for him to come to the Savior and a long period of disinterest may precede his decision. For Christ's sake we must love him nonetheless. It is the Holy Spirit, not we, who converts an individual. We, the privileged ambassadors of Jesus Christ, can communicate a verbal message; we can demonstrate through our personality and life what the grace of Jesus Christ can accomplish. But we must not go around chalking up scalps, taking credit for the Holy Spirit's work and saying, "I've got seven! You've only got three." Such stupid and ridiculous spiritual pride is nauseating. We have the *privilege* of being ambassadors. We ought to anticipate the possibility of reaping, of being the last link in a long chain, of inviting a person to receive the Savior. But let us never naively think that *we* have converted a soul and brought him to Jesus Christ. When someone says, "I've converted twelve people!" I think I know what he means. But I shake my head in amazement and wish that *he* knew a little more about what he meant. No one calls Jesus *Lord* except by the Holy Spirit.

And yet the tremendous privilege of presenting Jesus Christ is ours. We are His only representatives in a lost world that yearns for reality.

*We can escape traffic without camping in the safety zone*

# 4. What Is Our Message?

**A**N ambassador must effectively communicate a message. If he is unsure of that message, he'll never be an effective ambassador. Many Christians are ineffective ambassadors because they're not sure of the content of their message and are unable to communicate it understandably to others. For many, understanding the gospel is like understanding a mathematical problem. They hear the mathematical problem explained in class and clearly understand it as the professor goes through it. But, when a friend who cut the class asks them to explain the problem, they are at a loss to do it in terms that are clear enough for the friend to grasp. Many who have believed and understood the gospel for themselves are unable to articulate it clearly enough to another person so that they, too, might know and experience the same Lord.

Other people include many true, but irrelevant things, in presenting the gospel. As a consequence, many of their friends are confused. Still others have a clear grasp of the content of the message but have a vocabulary which is not understood by a biblically illiterate, pagan non-Christian. Some time ago a Christian student was driving along the highway in Pennsylvania with a non-Christian. They passed a sign that said, "Jesus saves." The non-Christian remarked very sincerely, "That's something I never thought of before. If Jesus is thrifty, I ought to be too!"

In communicating the gospel it is essential to realize that Christianity is not a philosophy or a way of life but a living person, Jesus Christ. Unless a non-Christian realizes the issue is his personal relationship to this person rather than what church he should belong to, what amusements he should not attend, etc., we will have failed. Not even the crucial question of whether the Bible is the Word of God is the central issue in salvation. Many Christians get stopped before they start by trying to prove that the Bible is the Word of God. It is enough to show that the Bible is a reliable historical document; and on this basis confront a person with the claims of Christ.[1] After trusting the Savior, it is only logical to adopt His position with reference to Scripture and this clearly is that it is the inspired Word of God.

The gospel, then, is Jesus Christ Himself—who He is, what He has done, and how He can be known in personal experience.

Because the gospel is about a person, there is no rigid and rote way in which it is to be presented. Whenever we are talking about a person rather than a formula, we always begin with that aspect of the person's appearance, character and personality that are the most relevant at the moment. If you have a blond brother who is studying chemistry at Harvard and you meet someone who is also studying at Harvard, you don't begin the conversation by saying, "I have a brother who is blond, is studying chemistry, and is at Harvard." Rather, you begin, "Oh, I have a brother who is at Harvard," and you may then go to the other facts as they are relevant. On the other hand, if you meet someone who is almost an identical twin to your brother, you wouldn't begin by saying that you have a brother who is studying chemistry. Rather you might say, "You look just like my brother," and then go on to other facts.

In the same way, when we are talking about the Lord Jesus Christ, it may be that at one time His resurrection is the most relevant aspect of His person and work. Another time it might be His death, another His diagnosis of human nature, and another time who He is. Eventually, we want to cover all the information in the gospel. We must be conversant with the basic facts about the Lord Jesus Christ that a person ought to know to become a

---

[1] See F. F. Bruce, *The New Testament Documents: Are They Reliable?* (Grand Rapids, Michigan, Wm. B. Eerdmans, 1954).

Christian, and it is imperative to know where these can be documented in the New Testament.

## Basic Facts

What are some of these facts? The following is a brief outline. It is by no means exhaustive, but it will at least give a framework on which to base our thinking and give us some basic facts from which we can move in presenting the gospel. It follows the principle of using our Lord's words where possible and using the clearest possible references to support the fact.

### 1. Who He Is

*He is fully God.* A number of New Testament references document this, but the following are among the clearest: John 5:18, John 10:10-30; and John 14:9. In presenting the claims of Christ, it is helpful to use the words of Jesus where possible as there are some who suggest that this is all they will accept. It is also important to use the clearest statements possible. The ones that *we know* involve a prediction or a claim to Deity may not be clear to a non-Christian, i.e. Genesis 3:15 as a promise of a Savior.

*He is fully man:* John 4:6 and John 11:35.

### 2. His Diagnosis of Human Nature

In Mark 7:1-23 Jesus says that sin is a basic disease which defiles us and cuts us off from God. It has a variety of symptoms which originate internally and not externally. It is helpful to define sin experientially rather than propositionally. Merely to tell someone that "all have sinned" doesn't usually "get to them." However, to describe sin in experiential terms finds almost everyone agreeing that this includes him. Sin is a word that does not communicate in our society today. People usually think of *My Sin* perfume by Lanvin or immorality of one kind or another. If they don't happen to be guilty of this kind of immorality, they become highly incensed because they do not see themselves as sinners in these terms. Sin, however, is a basic disease of rebellion against God, of going our way rather than His. The symptoms vary widely with different people. But the disease and its results are universal. We are separated from God like a leaf cut off from a stem. It is this separation as a result of our sin which is at the heart of our boredom, loneliness, moral weakness, lack of purpose, etc.

### 3. The Fact and Meaning of His Crucifixion

This is described in each of the four gospels. In Matthew 26:28 our Lord explicitly says that His death is "for the forgiveness of sins." Peter, who was one of our Lord's closest disciples and hence knew His mind very clearly, states it very transparently in I Peter 3:18, "For Christ also has once suffered for sins, the just for the unjust, that he might bring us to God." Jesus Christ took the sentence of death that belongs to us as a result of our having broken God's moral law. Having stepped into our place to receive the judgment, He can now freely offer us forgiveness and restore us to the relationship that God intended for us in creation.

### 4. The Fact and Meaning of His Resurrection

This also is recorded in each of the four gospels. Perhaps the most dramatic account is Luke 24:36-48. Here we have a record of our Lord's appearance to the disciples on the shore of the Sea of Galilee. They were frightened and supposed that they had seen a spirit, but our Lord in those classic words said, "handle me and see; for a spirit has not flesh and bones as you see that I have." Jesus Christ rose from the dead in bodily form validating His claim to Deity. And this single fact revolutionized the early Christians; they were frightened and defeated on Good Friday, but they launched the mighty Christian movement as a result of Easter Sunday. The implication of the resurrection for our time is that the Lord Jesus Christ is a living person today. He is alive and powerful to invade the life of any person who invites Him into his life. And it is this resurrection power, available today, that makes Christianity unique.

### 5. Becoming a Christian

A person needs to know how to come to know Jesus Christ personally for himself. It is at this point that many who know the facts are unable to communicate clearly. We use vague, abstract terms like believe, have faith, etc., which do not describe concretely what is involved in becoming a Christian. It seems to me that the clearest statement in the New Testament on how to become a Christian is John 1:12, "To as many as received him to them gave he the power to become the children of God, even to them that believe on his name." There are three operative verbs in this statement: *believe, receive, become.* Somone has said that in becoming a Christian there is *something* to be believed and *someone* to be received. This aptly sums up this verse.

It is significant that marriage is one of the illustrations the New Testament uses for being and becoming a Christian. It is obvious that merely believing in a fellow or a girl, however intense that belief might be, does not make one married. If, in addition, we are emotionally involved and have that "all gone feeling" about the other person we still will not be married! One finally has to come to a commitment of the will and say, "I do," receiving the other person into his life and committing himself to the other person thereby establishing a relationship. It involves total commitment of intellect, emotions and will. One must believe in Jesus Christ; and personally receive Him into one's life; and thus become a child of God. The pattern is the same in marriage: a fellow first believes in a girl, then must receive her into his life and thus become married.

Mere intellectual assent to facts does not make a person a Christian any more than mere intellectual assent to facts makes a person married. Many people's dissatisfaction with Chrisitianity is because they are like a person who says, "I believe in marriage, I'm sold on marriage, I've read a dozen books on marriage and in the last three months I've been to 15 weddings, but for some strange reason marriage doesn't mean anything to me." The reason is very simple: he isn't married. Marriage is not a philosophy number 67 as opposed to singlehood 12. Nor is Christianity a philosophy number 78 as opposed to existentialism 3, agnosticism 14 or logical positivism 21. Rather it is a dynamic relationship with a living person, the Lord Jesus Christ. Just as getting married means giving up our independence, so does receiving Christ. The essence of sin is living independently of God—going my way rather than His way. The essence of repentance is the repudiation of this self-centered principle making Christ and His will the center of my life. When we marry, we must think of another person in all our decisions. When we receive Christ, we enter into a consultative relationship with Him about every area of our lives. Our first thought must be: what does He think and desire?

How then does one actually receive Jesus Christ? In Revelation 3:20 Jesus Christ compares our lives to a house and says, "Behold I stand at the door and knock. If any man hears my voice and opens the door, I will come in to him and eat with him and he with me." Showing him this verse, I often ask an interested student, "Suppose someone came to the door of your room and knocked. How would you get the person inside?" The student thinks for a moment and then says, "Why I'd open the door." I say, "Exactly. And then what would you do?" Invariably they respond, "I'd invite the person in." Usually a flash of insight crosses their face as they realize that this is exactly how one becomes a Christian. The Lord Jesus Christ is knocking at the door of our lives. He will not gate-crash or force His way in but will come in at our invitation. This invitation can be given Him simply in our own words in prayer. And when we receive Him, He promises to come in and be with us for eternity.

## Basic Pattern

Not only do we need the basic facts of the gospel so that we may range freely over them, we also need a format in which we may present the gospel (assuming an opportunity arises without obstruction or objection). I find a three-phase pattern very helpful. In conversation it is usually possible to get people to agree that there is something wrong with the world. The next step is to discuss the *diagnosis* of what is wrong, realizing that unless an accurate diagnosis can be given no dynamic cure can ever be reached. The Lord Jesus Christ gives the diagnosis that man is suffering from the disease of sin which has separated him from his Maker. He says this is the basic reason we suffer all the frustrations, problems, loneliness, and boredom that we see all around us. The solution to these problems and many others is the restoration of this relationship; we then come to the prescription for the cure: the Lord Jesus Christ. This format: the problem, the diagnosis and the cure can be useful in getting right to the point.

As we have observed, we are living in a pagan and biblically illiterate society. For this reason we need to be particularly careful to guard against what Eugene Nida calls "Protestant Latin." In a recent survey it was discovered that 74% of the school children in New York were unable to correctly identify the first four books of the Bible. We will probably be deeply disappointed if we assume our listener has biblical knowledge and understanding. We must be able to clearly define terms which have great meaning to us but very little meaning to pagans, such as, born again, regeneration,

salvation, saved, propitiation, sanctification, justification. What do
we actually mean by these words? The best way is to sit down and
write out a definition without using the word itself.

## Three Steps

How can we improve our knowledge and understanding of
the message? Here are a few practical steps. First, write out the
gospel to a hypothetical friend who has no objections, but is ig-
norant of the gospel. Ask a non-Christian to read over what you
have written and ask him what he understands it to say. This will
help you see if you are communicating and also give you the opportunity to impart the gospel to a non-Christian.

Secondly, you could explain the gospel to a friend who is a
Christian and practice verbalizing the gospel to someone who is
sympathetic. Third, try to verbalize the good news to a stranger,
even suggesting the fact that you are trying to learn to communicate
and you would appreciate his help. Again, you would have an
opportunity to witness and would quickly find the weaknesses in
your thinking and communication. The only guarantee we are communicating clearly is when the other person can give back what has
been said in terms that we can recognize.

Every Christian is a witness and an ambassador, as witnesses
and ambassadors we must know our message clearly.

*"As you were saying, Mr. Ambassador."*

# 5. Why We Believe

I

N our time it's not enough to know what we believe as Christians, we must also know *why* we believe it. Every Christian should be able to defend his faith. This is a spiritual responsibility about which we are clearly instructed in I Peter 3:15: "But in your hearts reverence Christ as Lord. Always be prepared to make a defense to any one who calls you to account for the hope that is in you, yet do it with gentleness and reverence."

This command is not optional. We can see good, practical reasons for it. First, for the sake of our own conviction about the truth, we should have an answer ready. Unless we are fully persuaded in our own minds that Jesus Christ is the truth, we will never effectively communicate the gospel to anyone else. Moreover, our own spiritual lives will soon become impoverished. One cannot drive himself indefinitely to do with his will something about which he is not intellectually convinced: emotional collapse sets in. We ourselves must be convinced of the truth.

Second, we have a responsibility to help the thoughtful non-Christian with his honest questions about Christianity. If we are constantly allowing non-Christians to silence us with their questions, we are confirming them in their unbelief. I'm not suggesting that it's impossible for us to witness effectively about Jesus Christ if we don't have answers. We can always fall back on the fact of our own experience, as the blind man in John 9 did. When he was asked a great many questions he couldn't answer, he told his critics, "One thing I know, that though I was blind, now I see" (verse 25). When we don't know the answers to all the questions put to us, we can always stand squarely on what we do know: that Jesus Christ has changed our lives. However, this should not be our only recourse. We are responsible for mastering the answers to repeatedly asked questions.

## Two Harmful Attitudes

In considering and answering the questions non-Christians ask, we need to avoid two opposite but equally harmful attitudes. The first is basically an anti-intellectual attitude. Some people assert, "You don't have to bother with the wisdom of men. Don't even try to think out Christianity." They imply that it's wrong to try to work ideas through. "Don't get sidetracked by people's questions. Just preach the simple gospel." The tragic result of accepting such a view is that many thinking non-Christians conclude from our behavior that their honest questions have no answers. And we sometimes begin to wonder ourselves whether or not we have the truth: if we faced the facts as they really are, would our faith hold water? The anti-intellectual attitude is usually a dead-end street for both the non-Christian and for us.

Second, we must guard against a naive reliance on the answers we have, as though answers themselves will bring people to Jesus Christ. Sometimes we tend to think that any explanation that makes sense to us and has helped a few others is a magic wand. We think we'll go out and wow people with it, so they'll have no choice except to believe. Of course, we're naive in thinking this, for we've already noted that no man calls Jesus, Lord, except by the Holy Spirit. Unless the Holy Spirit illumines a person's mind to see the truth as truth, unless He bends that person's proud will to submit to the authority of Jesus Christ, no words of ours will penetrate. But in the hands of God an intelligent answer to a person's question may well be the instrument that opens his heart and mind to the gospel. We must recognize the spiritual warfare in which we and the questioner are involved. Paul explained the reason that people do not believe: ". . . the god of this world has blinded the minds of the unbelievers, to keep them from seeing the light of the gospel of the glory of Christ" (II Corinthians 4:4). Information cannot bring them to the truth unless a supernatural work also occurs to enlighten them. Often God and the Holy Spirit do use a presentation of information as an instrument to bring someone to faith in Jesus Christ.

## Cater to Intellectual Integrity

John Stott, rector of All Souls, Langham Place, London, struck the proper balance in his statement: "We cannot pander to a man's intellectual arrogance, but we must cater to his intellectual integrity." The whole man, including his intellect and emotions and will, must be converted. If we simply convert the intellect, but do not convert the will, we won't have a Christian. In chapter 4 we considered the inadequacy of a mere mental assent to propositions. On the other hand, an emotional assent to Christ, divorced from mind and will, would again mean an incomplete conversion. The total personality—intellect, emotions, and will—must be converted.

I would be the last one to suggest that we as Christians have all the answers to the problems of the world, or even all the answers to the problems in Christianity. By no means! The French philosopher and mathematician, Pascal, pointed out that the supreme function of reason is to show man that some things are beyond reason. However, our Lord, referring to Himself, said, "And you will know the truth, and the truth will make you free" (John 8:32). Surely He meant that we do have some absolutes on which to base our lives and destiny. Without these absolutes, we have very little as Christians to offer today's world.

I am disturbed by an attitude that I sometimes discover among Christians as well as non-Christians: the suggestion that the *pursuit* of truth is all that really counts. People don't really want any answers because that would end their game. For them, the pursuit of truth is everything. Truth itself is less attractive—a fact they often rationalize as: truth is unattainable. As a result they equate almost any answer with a pat or contrived answer. This, to me, is dangerous thinking. An answer that is valid is not necessarily pat. "Patness" is betrayed by the attitude in which an answer is given. A pat answer comes out like the recorded song that plays when you put a nickel in the slot. The answer which takes into consideration the background of the questioner and his question and which cogently addresses itself to the point is not a pat answer. We can't alter the facts to make them fit someone's presuppositions, but we can present them as a challenge to his intellectual integrity. Let's not shy away from an honest declaration of the truth which we have received.

## Four Ph.D.'s Are Not Necessary

When we think about people's questions, we often let the mass of information we haven't mastered overwhelm us. Before we can give effective answers, we think we'll need to get four Ph.D.'s and a reading knowledge of 5,000 books. We may get breathless just thinking about this hopeless task. Then we conclude, "I can't do it. I guess this isn't my area of witnessing." However, as I've been privileged to speak to hundreds of audiences of non-Christians on almost two hundred secular campuses, here and abroad, I've learned that this isn't the case. When I began, I thought I'd never survive. My first evangelistic discussion some years ago was at the University of Kansas in—of all places—a scholarship hall. I thought, "Lord, why must I begin in one of these residences reserved for brainy students on scholarship? They'll tear me apart from limb-to-limb!" Although I didn't expect to live through that night, I did, by the grace of God and His goodness; and moreover a fellow became a Christian that evening and is faithfully serving Jesus Christ today. That night I began to acquire some valuable information. I discovered some of the questions non-Christians have on their minds. As I traveled to other campuses and spoke more and more with students, a pattern emerged in the questions they asked me.

In any aspect of life, all of us fear the unknown. Why don't we like to do door-to-door knocking? Some of us get the shakes just thinking about it. We're afraid because we don't know what's behind the door. Why do people fear death, basically? Until we receive Jesus Christ, death is a great unknown to us. Any experience that involves the unknown is difficult. Leading my first few discussions was a major problem for me because I didn't know what to expect. But now I can predict, with a very high degree of accuracy, the questions that will be asked me in any given discussion with non-Christians. A few of the questions may depart from the pattern, but most of them will fit into one of several basic categories.

Incidentally, I recently held a mock bull session with students on a Christian college campus. They wanted to set up a typical fraternity situation so we assumed that they were the fraternity men and I'd come in to speak. I talked to them a while the way I usually do in a fraternity and then let them ask me whatever they wanted to. I think it's rather significant that they asked all kinds of questions that I've never been asked in my fifteen years of visiting secular campuses. Many of their questions were weighted in Christian theological terms or involved issues like the apparent discrepancies in the Scripture. Most non-Christians on a secular campus are biblically illiterate and so they ask more basic questions. This comparison indicates that the mind of the average student in a Christian school and the mind of the average non-Christian student tend to run in different channels. While this difference is understandable, it creates a problem for Christians trying to relate to non-Christians. We need to know the answers to the questions non-Christians are actually asking, rather than to be boned up on a dozen things they may never ask about. If we have the right answers to the wrong questions, we aren't much help.

At the University of Georgia recently, one of the fellows on our team was really impressed by the way certain questions kept coming up. He had read my short articles reprinted from *His* magazine, "What Non-Christians Ask," and he remarked, "You know it's absolutely uncanny. I've been in three fraternities so far this week, and practically every one of these questions has come up every time!" Thus his first experience in actual face-to-face confrontation with non-Christians' questions confirmed the pattern. Because there is a pattern to the questions we'll be asked, we don't have to go out and amass mountains of information. If we think through the answers to the common, basic questions we'll acquire confidence and be able to help those who are asking these questions.

## Seven Basic Questions

Again and again on the secular campus, I've been asked seven basic questions—sometimes with slight variations on the theme. I'd like to suggest briefly some of the answers I've given. You can undoubtedly improve them.

### 1. What About the Heathen?

Non-Christians, and many Christians too, most frequently ask about the heathen. "What about the person who has never heard of Jesus Christ? Will he be condemned to hell?" At the outset I think we must acknowledge that we don't have the whole story about how God will deal with these people. He hasn't told us. Certain things are known to God alone. In Deuteronomy 29:29 we read, "The secret things belong to the Lord our God; but the things that are revealed belong to us and to our children for ever." On some things God has not fully revealed His plan; this is one instance. Our concern is to be with the things He has revealed. As we think about this question, however, Scripture does offer some very clear points for us to keep in mind.

*First,* God is just. All the evidence we have indicates that we can have confidence in His character. We can trust that whatever He does with those who have never heard of Jesus Christ will be fair. All our data indicates that God's character is just.

*Second,* no person will be condemned for rejecting Jesus Christ of whom he has never heard; instead, he will be condemned for violating his own moral standard, however high or low it has been. The whole world—every person, whether he has heard of the Ten Commandments or not—is in sin. Romans 2 clearly tells us that every person has a standard of some kind, and that in every culture, people knowingly violate the standard they have. A knowledge of anthropology confirms this. Paul writes:

> *All who have sinned without knowledge of the Law will die without reference to the Law: and all who have sinned knowing the Law shall be judged according to the Law. It is not familiarity with the Law that justifies a man in the sight of God, but obedience to it.*
>
> *When the gentiles, who have no knowledge of the Law, act in accordance with it by the light of nature, they show that they have a law in themselves, for they demonstrate the effect of a law operating in their own hearts. Their own consciences endorse the existence of such a law, for there is something which condemns or excuses their actions.*
>
> *We may be sure that all this will be taken into account in the day of true judgment, when God will judge men's secret lives by Christ Jesus, as my gospel plainly states. Romans 2:12-16*[1]

---

[1] *The New Testament in Modern English,* trans. by J. B. Phillips (New York, The Macmillan Company, 1958). Quoted by permission of the Macmillan Company and Geoffrey Bles LTD., publishers, London.

*Third,* Scripture indicates that every man has enough information from creation to know that God exists. This is clearly stated in Romans 1:19, 20: "For what can be known about God is plain to them, because God has shown it to them. Ever since the creation of the world his invisible nature, namely his eternal power and deity, has been clearly perceived in the things that have been made. So they are without excuse." Psalm 19 confirms this fact. From Matthew 7:7-11 and Jeremiah 29:13 we may conclude that if a man responds to the light he has and seeks God, God will give him a chance to hear the truth about Jesus Christ.

*Fourth,* there is no indication in the Bible that a man can be saved apart from Jesus Christ. This is made crystal clear. Our Lord Himself declared in John 14:6, "I am the way, and the truth, and the life; no one comes to the Father, but by me." Jesus spoke with the authority of God. Because of who He is and what He has done on the cross, it is obvious that there is no other way to God. Only He atoned for our sins. He is the only bridge across the chasm that separates the highest possible human achievement from the infinitely holy standard of God. Peter left no room for doubt in his flat assertion in Acts 4:12, "And there is salvation in no one else, for there is no other name under heaven given among men by which we must be saved." This places tremendous responsibility on us who call ourselves Christians; we must see to it that those who have not heard hear the gospel.

The *final* thing to point out to the person who has raised this question is the Bible's absolute clarity concerning the judgment which awaits the individual who has heard the gospel, as this person has. When he faces God, the issue will not be the heathen. He will have to account for what he personally has done with Jesus Christ. Usually someone will raise the question of the heathen as a smoke screen so he can evade his personal responsibility. We need to answer this question for him. We also need to think it through for our conviction and confidence. But then, as we terminate the discussion, we should focus on the person himself and on his responsibility: What is *he* going to do with Jesus Christ? *The Case for Christianity* by C. S. Lewis contains a fuller discussion of the moral law inherent in the universe.

## 2. Is Christ the Only Way to God?

The second question, which is a corollary or slight variation of the first, is this: 'Doesn't the sincere Moslem or Buddhist or Hindu worship the same God as the Christian, but under a different name?" In other words, "Is Jesus Christ really the only way to God?"

Neither sincerity nor intensity of faith can create truth. Faith is no more valid than the object in which it is placed. Believing doesn't make something true, per se, and refusing to believe a truth cannot make it false. The real issue is the question of truth. Let's compare Islam and Christianity as an example. In the moral and ethical realms we can find many similarities between them, but the two faiths are diametrically opposed on the most crucial question: Who is Jesus Christ? Islam denies that Jesus Christ is God the Son. It denies that He died on the cross and rose from the dead. Christianity, on the other hand, affirms and focuses upon the fact that Jesus Christ, the Son of God, died on the cross for our sin and then rose from the dead. Both faiths cannot simultaneously be true at this particular point. One is correct; one is incorrect. If the crux of Christianity is false, our faith is worthless.

This question about other religions has some emotional aspects which we need to try to overcome when we discuss it. We want people to realize that Christians are not being bigoted and prejudiced or presumptuous when they say that Christ is the only way to God. As Christians we have no other option because Jesus Christ Himself has said this. Although one may choose to believe whatever he wishes, he has no right to redefine Christianity in his own terms. If we're going to be faithful to Jesus Christ we must take our stand on what He said. Quite obviously, if He is God this is the only answer. Acknowledging this, no one should feel that if we were only less bigoted our "fraternity" could get together and change its membership rules. That suggestion misses the point altogether. We're dealing with truth that has come to us by revelation, through the invasion into human history of God Himself in Jesus Christ.

An illustration has often helped to make this point clear. In some areas of life, the penalties for breaking laws are socially determined. For instance, there's a stop sign on the corner. By vote the community can decide on a $5, $10, or $50 fine for going through that sign. Or it can abolish the fine. The penalty is not determined by the act of going through the stop sign; the legal penalty is not inherent in the violation. But in some other aspects of life, such as in the physical realm, we find laws that are not socially determined. Suppose our community passed a unanimous resolution to suspend the law of gravity an hour a day, from 8:00 to 9:00 A.M. Who would join me in jumping off the roof to try it out? Suppose we passed the resolution three times? I still wouldn't get any takers. We do not determine socially the penalty for violating the law of gravity; the penalty is inherent in the violation. Even if we passed motions till the cows came home, the fact would remain that if you jumped off the roof someone would have to pick you up with a shovel! In the moral realm, as in the physical, there are laws that are not socially determined. We discern these laws from what God has revealed about the inherent law of the universe. Dorothy L. Sayers offers some further helpful thoughts on this subject in *The Mind of the Maker*.

### 3. Why Do the Innocent Suffer?

The third frequently asked question concerns the problem of evil. "If God is all-good and all-powerful, why do the innocent suffer? Why are some babies born blind or mentally defective or deformed? Why are wars allowed? Why . . .?" Either God is all-good, but He is not powerful enough to eliminate disease and disaster; or He is all-powerful, but He is not all-good and therefore He does not end all evil. Once again I think we must admit our partial ignorance. We don't have the full explanation of the origin and problem of evil because God has chosen to reveal only a part of it to us. We are clearly told, though, that God created the universe perfect. Man was given the freedom to obey God or disobey. Evil came into the universe through man's disobedience. Because of the pattern of the universe, man's actions are not limited to himself but always involve other people. Because man disobeyed and broke God's law, evil pervades the universe.

As we discuss this question, we mustn't overlook the presence of evil in every one of us. Many people ask, "Why doesn't God step in and get rid of evil? Why doesn't He stomp out war?" They do not realize that if God executed judgment uniformly, not one of us would survive. Suppose God were to decree, "At midnight tonight all evil will be stamped out of the universe." Which of us would be here at 1:00 A.M.?

After we point out man's personal problem with evil we need to note that God has done everything necessary to meet the problem of evil. He not only came into human history in the Lord Jesus Christ, but He died to solve the problem of evil. Every individual who willingly responds receives His gift of love, grace, and forgiveness in Jesus Christ. As C. S. Lewis has observed, it is idle for us to speculate about the origin of evil. The problem we all face is the *fact* of evil. The only solution to the fact of evil is God's solution, Jesus Christ.

### 4. How Can Miracles Be Possible?

Question number four asks about miracles and opposes naturalism to supernaturalism. "How can miracles be possible? In this scientific age, how can any intelligent person who considers the orderliness of the universe believe in them?" If we don't get to the root of this question, we may waste long hours discussing whether Christ could possibly have walked on the water, whether in fact He did feed the five thousand with five loaves and two fish, whether the children of Israel actually went through the Red Sea, et cetera. We can only answer this question if we dig down to its basic presupposition. The real issue is whether or not God exists. If God exists, then miracles are logical and pose no intellectual contradictions. A Japanese friend once told me he just couldn't quite believe that a man could become God. I saw his problem in a flash and said, "Dr. Fukuma, I'd have quite a time believing that, too. But I can very easily believe that God became man." There's all the difference in the world between these two concepts. By definition God is all-powerful. He can and does intervene in the universe that He has created.

Ultimately we're being asked, "How do I know God exists?" Various answers will suggest the existence of God. One is the argument from design. If my wrist watch, relatively uncomplicated as it is, doesn't exist "by chance," it seems illogical and naive to think that the universe in its infinite intricacy could have developed just "by chance." A similar argument is based on the law of cause and effect. As human beings if we have intellect, emotion, and will, we assume that there was a cause greater than these to bring us into being. However, these answers have counter arguments and some evidence seems to negate them. So we should regard them as hints rather than conclusive proof that God exists.

The greatest indication of the existence of God is His coming into human history. As J. B. Phillips put it, we are "the visited planet." In answering any one of these questions, we must eventually come to the same solution: Jesus Christ Himself. I know God exists, not because of all the philosophical arguments pro and con, but because He came into human history in Jesus Christ and I have met Him personally in my own life. Our answer begins with Him. Because Jesus Christ claims to be God, we should ask ourselves whether His credentials substantiate His claim. Anyone, after all, can make the claim. I can; you can. A man in Philadelphia claims to be God and calls himself "Father Divine." But with what credentials does one substantiate his claim? I dare say I could disprove your claim in five minutes, and you could probably disprove mine in two. And it's not hard to disprove the claim of our friend in Philadelphia. But when we consider Jesus Christ it's not so simple. His credentials do substantiate His claim. The supreme credential, of course, is the fact that He rose from the dead.

In helping a non-Christian think through the intellectual basis of Christianity our best defense is a good offense. We don't want to be answering questions all the time. We can pose a few questions for him, too. Since he doesn't believe, *he* has some questions to answer. One way to stimulate his thinking is to ask, "Which of the other three possibilities about Jesus Christ do you believe since you don't believe He was the Truth?" There are only four possible conclusions about Jesus Christ and His claims. He was either a liar, a lunatic, a legend, or the Truth. The person who doesn't believe He was the Truth must label Him as a liar, a lunatic, or a legend. The average non-Christian doesn't realize this. So we've got to remind him that by saying he doesn't believe, he's left himself only three alternatives.

"Which conclusion do you believe, and what evidence can you present to support this conclusion? Was he a liar?" Even those who deny His deity will invariably hasten to assure us that Jesus was a great moral philosopher and teacher. To call this good teacher a liar would be a contradiction of terms. It certainly seems improbable that He would lie about the most crucial point in His teaching, His deity.

Perhaps he was a lunatic. This conclusion would not destroy His moral integrity: He thought He was doing right, but He suffered from delusions of grandeur. We have people like this today who imagine they are Napoleon, or even Jesus Christ. The hitch in this conclusion is that the clinical symptoms of paranoia as we know it today don't jibe with the personality characteristics of Jesus Christ. In His life we find no trace of the imbalance that characterizes such people. Consider the time of His death, for instance, when He was under tremendous pressure. The poise and composure we see in Him are not characteristic of people who suffer from paranoid disturbances. The biblical record gives no evidence that He was suffering from paranoia or any other mental disorder.

A third alternative is that our records about Jesus Christ are legendary. He never made some of the statements attributed to Him. They were put into His mouth by over-enthusiastic followers in the third or fourth century. He'd turn over in His grave if He knew the claims that have been written about Him. Modern archaeology, however, makes it increasingly difficult to maintain this theory. For instance, recent findings confirm the belief that the New Testament documents were written during the life-time of contemporaries of Jesus Christ. The development of an elaborate legend would have required a more significant time lag. People in that skeptical age would have been no more likely to circulate and accept a legend such as this than our neighbors today would be likely to spread a report that the late President Franklin D. Roosevelt claimed to be God, said he had the power to forgive sins, and rose from the dead. Too many people who knew President Roosevelt are still around. With so many testimonies to the contrary, the rumor could never get off the ground.

In discussing the existence of God, we also need to consider with the person what it means to prove or not prove God. Without realizing it, he probably expects proof according to the scientific method. We can never prove God by the scientific method. But this doesn't mean that our case is lost. The scientific method as a means of verification is limited to measurable aspects of reality. The scientific method, therefore, is incapable of verifying many aspects of life. No one has ever seen three feet of love or two pounds of justice, but we do not deny their reality. To insist that everything must be subjected to the scientific method for verification would be as ludicrous as to insist on measuring chlorine gas with a microphone. That's not the purpose of the microphone; we can't make it do what it has no capacity to do and deny the reality of gas in the process!

Another limitation of the scientific method is the need to

verify a fact through repetition; such repetition is part of the scientific method. Now history happens to be nonrepeatable. Since no one is ever going to repeat Napoleon, we can emphatically say that we can't prove Napoleon—by the scientific method, that is. But what does that prove? Nothing much. Because we can't repeat history, it's outside the scope of the scientific method of verification. However, there is a science of history. As we examine the data for Christianity, and particularly the evidence for the resurrection, we find a solid case on which to base our conviction.

These are the ideas we need to suggest to a person who takes the essentially materialistic position based on rationalistic presuppositions and claims that because there is no supernatural, miracles are impossible. When someone begins with this presupposition, no amount of evidence will convince him of the truth. If you started out by denying that miracles are possible, what evidence would convince you that a miracle had taken place? None. People who say, "if God would appear to me now I'd believe in Him," are very naive. Regardless of what happened, they'd explain it away in non-miraculous, naturalistic terms. Christ dealt with this problem in Luke 16:28-31, where the rich man in hell asked Abraham to send Lazarus to warn his brothers. Abraham reminded him, "They have Moses and the prophets; let them hear them." But the rich man said, "No, father Abraham; but if some one goes to them from the dead, they will repent." Abraham told him, "If they do not hear Moses and the prophets, neither will they be convinced if some one should rise from the dead." The principle still holds today. The data we have concerning God's visitation to this planet are sufficient grounds for us to believe. When someone refuses to accept this evidence, no additional evidence will convince him.

## 5. Isn't the Bible Full of Errors?

The fifth question starts out, "How do you reconcile your faith with the fact that the Bible is so full of errors?" The reliability of Scripture is being challenged. At the outset we need to ask what particular errors the person has in mind. Ninety-nine per cent of the time people can't think of any. They've heard someone else say that the Bible is full of contradictions and they've swallowed the assumption. But sometimes a person has a specific problem in mind. If you don't have the answer to his particular question, don't panic. Instead smile casually and tell him, "I don't have the answer to that one, but I'll be glad to dig it up for you." Volumes have been written on some of these topics. After two thousand years, no one this week is going to think of the question that will bring Christianity crashing down.

If the person hasn't read the Bible, that's a fair indication of his insincerity in questioning it. But don't press this point with him. Under no circumstances should we make fun of anyone or try to argue by ridicule. This is deadly behavior when we're talking to someone about these important issues. Some of the greatest damage to the Christian faith has been caused by those who, though meaning well, attempted to win their case by ridiculing the other person's position. They only brought the gospel into disrepute.

The Bible does contain some apparent contradictions. However, our friend probably doesn't realize that time and time again an apparent contradiction has been vindicated by the discoveries of modern archaeology. Dr. Nelson Glueck, an outstanding Jewish archaeologist, makes the remarkable statement, "No archaeological discovery has ever controverted a biblical reference."[2] And this phenomenal statement comes from one of the world's leading archaeologists. For those still unreconciled conflicts between the Bible and history, our logical attitude.should be to wait and see what further evidence will disclose. We don't have all the answers to all the problems. But all the vindicating data thus far certainly suggest that we can trust the biblical record about those details that still appear questionable.

Evolution is a problem in evangelism only insofar as it leads to an atheistic conclusion. It is unwise to get involved in a technical discussion about evolution because it isn't the real issue. I usually ask, "What conclusion are you drawing from your evolutionary position—that the universe happened by chance? Or are you saying that God created the universe and did so by using certain evolutionary processes? I'm not convinced about that particular position, but let's assume for the moment it's correct. What conclusion are you drawing?" From there I direct his attention to what Jesus Christ has said and done. *How* God brought the universe into being is not so important as *that* He did it. One's presupposition and not the actual evidence often determines his conclusion. If the person is trying to suggest that God is not the author of creation

---

[2] Nelson Glueck, *Rivers in the Desert* (New York, Grove Press, 1960), p. 31.

and that the universe did happen by chance, then we need to discuss this problem with him. An apparently strong case for a naturalistic position can be made by ignoring the evidence for Jesus Christ. But if a person is going to be intellectually honest, he must come to grips with Him. An amazing number of thinking non-Christians have never really thought about the evidence for Jesus Christ.

## 6. Isn't Christian Experience Only Psychological?

The sixth question is subtle and can become rather personal: "Isn't it possible to explain Christian experience in purely psychological terms?" Some people suggest that we have faith only because we've been conditioned, since our early childhood, to this way of thinking and living. They think we've been raised like Pavlov's dogs. But they oversimplify the situation. Anyone who has traveled widely and met other Christians knows that preconditioning can't explain many conversions, for Christians have been converted from every imaginable background. Thousands of them had no childhood contact with Christianity. Yet each one will testify that a personal encounter with Jesus Christ transformed his life. In his studies, the psychologist tries to keep all but one or two factors constant. To verify his conclusion he must eliminate as many variables as possible. But in comparing the lives of Christians, the Lord Himself is the only constant factor. From one case history to the next all other details may vary. Only He remains the same. He alone in His power makes a thief honest, a profligate pure, a liar truthful. It is He who can fill a hate-ridden heart with love.

Other psychology-minded people assert that ideas of spiritual reality are essentially wish fulfillments. All religious experience, they contend, can be traced to man's feeling a need for God, creating an image in his mind, and then worshiping the mental projection. His supposed spiritual reality, of course, lacks any objective reality. Again and again we hear religion called the crutch of people who can't get along in life. This view raises a valid issue which we must consider.

How can we know that we haven't hypnotized ourselves into believing what we want to believe? If our spiritual experience is just a result of wish fulfillment or positive thinking, we should be able to regard any object, an organ for instance, as God. If we think about the organ as God long enough it will become God to us; then lo and behold, we've a subjective experience. But what is our objective evidence for this subjective experience?

Let's try another situation. Suppose someone wanders into your room with a fried egg dangling over his left ear and says, "Man, this fried egg is the most! I get joy, peace, satisfaction, and purpose in life from it. Tremendous, man—this fried egg is really it." What do you say? In the final analysis you can't argue with experience. That's why a Christian's testimony is so effective; no one can argue with it. And you can't argue experimentally with this fried-egg guy.

But you can investigate his experience by asking him several crucial questions (the same questions that every Christian should' be prepared to answer about his experience). How do you know it's the fried egg and not auto-hypnosis that's giving you this satisfaction and peace? Who else has gotten the same benefits out of the egg? To what objective fact is this experience tied? Christianity differs from auto-hypnosis, wish fulfillments, and all the other psychological phenomena in that the Christian's subjective experience is securely bound to an objective, historical fact, namely the resurrection from the dead of Jesus Christ.

A professor in semantics from the University of California in Berkeley recently attended a series of meetings where I was the speaker. He was a complete relativist in his thinking. Right in the middle of my talks he would stand up in the audience and interpret (and briefly refute) what I had said. I'll admit it was all done in good spirit, but it was a bit unnerving, too. He advanced the popular idea that what we believe is true to us but not necessarily true for other people, and he used this illustration: A man may be tied on a railroad track in a fraternity hazing. When the train whizzes by on the next track, he dies of a heart attack because he doesn't know that it's not on his track. As far as he's concerned the train might as well have been on the first track. He believed it was and so it became true for him. You see, what's true for you may not be true for me. Time and time again we tried to show this professor the significant difference in Christianity, the fact of the resurrection. About the fourth time around the penny dropped. Standing at the blackboard with a piece of chalk in his hand, he suddenly stopped in the middle of a sentence and said, "Hmm . . ., yes, that would make quite a difference," and sat down.

If the resurrection is true, it makes all the difference in the world. It is confirmation of God's revelation in Christ, an absolute truth, an historical fact outside of ourselves, an objective fact to which our subjective experience is tied. We need to hold these two facts, the objective and the subjective, in proper perspective. The fact that Jesus Christ rose from the dead means nothing to me personally or experientially until I receive Him as Lord and Savior in my own life. On the other hand, if I have only my own experience, I'll sooner or later begin wondering if it is real or merely self-suggestion. I need to recognize that my experience is based on the solid foundation of an objective fact in history.

For a brief and helpful summary, read the Inter-Varsity Press booklet, *Evidence for the Resurrection* by J. N. D. Anderson, a professor of oriental law at London University. He discusses the evidence and the various alternatives that have been advanced to explain away the resurrection, showing why, in the light of the data, each explanation is inadequate.

## 7. Won't a Good Moral Life Get Me to Heaven?

The seventh question reflects a very prevalent attitude of our age. "Isn't living a good moral life all I need to do to get to heaven?" Or as a student at Duke University said after a discussion, "If God grades on the curve, I'll make it." His words are an apt summary of the confusion today about religion in general. Most people will accept this philosophy that all we need to do is our best, and then everything will be all right, or at least we'll be able to squeak by. In this wistful dream hope we see an incredible optimism about man's righteousness and an appalling ignorance of God's infinite holiness. God doesn't grade on the curve. He has an absolute standard, Jesus Christ.

Light, when it is turned on, destroys darkness. Likewise, the character of God so blazes in its purity that it consumes all evil. As we are, we could not abide in His presence, but would be consumed because of the corruption in our lives. The perfect righteousness of Jesus Christ is the only basis on which we can come into fellowship with the living God.

An illustration helps people to see their misunderstanding here. Suppose the entire human race lined up on the West Coast with one objective, to get to Hawaii. We'll equate their goal with God's standard of righteousness. The gun is fired and all the swimmers jump in. As we look down over the ocean we see the most moral of all. He's been a wonderful professor and a good man, always doing his best and following high moral standards; yet he would be the first to admit his imperfection and sinfulness. But he's out there in the water seventy-five miles from shore. Next we pick out the Joe College fellow who's not quite ready for Sing-Sing or Cook County Jail. He does cheat on exams a little and goes on a binge now and then; he gets into a few scrapes and does things that are wrong. But he's not really too bad. He's gotten about ten miles out. A derelict from Skid Row is practically drowning one hundred and fifty yards offshore. Scattered about in the water between the two extremes of the spectrum we see the rest of the human race. As we look from the bum on Skid Row to the Joe College type to the tremendously moral man who's gone seventy-five miles, we see the difference. It's an enormous difference. But what's the difference in terms of Hawaii? Everyone will drown.

A set of swimming instructions won't help at this point. We need somebody who will take us to Hawaii. This is where Jesus Christ comes in. If you can make it to Hawaii by yourself, if you can live a life that is absolutely perfect in thought, word, and deed, you can make it to heaven on your own steam. But no man ever has or ever will succeed. All the other religions of the world are essentially sets of swimming instructions, suggested codes of ethics for a wonderful pattern of life. But man's basic problem is not knowing *how* he ought to live; it is lacking the *power* to live as he ought. The good news of Christianity is that Jesus Christ, who invaded human history, does for us what we couldn't possibly do for ourselves. Through Him we may be reconciled to God, given His righteousness, and enabled to have fellowship with Him in His very presence.

## Basic Problem Is Moral

Now that we've briefly thought through these seven questions, we need to be reminded that ultimately man's basic problem is not intellectual; it's moral. Once in a while our answer won't satisfy someone. His rejection of the answer doesn't invalidate it. On the other hand, he may be convinced and still not become a Christian. I've had fellows tell me, "You've answered every one of my questions to my satisfaction." After thanking them for the flattery I've asked, "Are you going to become a Christian then?" and they've smiled a little sheepishly, "Well, no." "Why not?" I've inquired. "Frankly, it would mean too radical a change in my way of life." Many people are not prepared to let anyone else, including God, run their lives. It's not that they *can't* believe; but they *won't* believe. They at least see what the issue is. Our responsibility in using the information in this chapter is to help them reach this point of understanding.

People often ask, "If Christianity is true, why do the majority of intelligent people not believe it?" The answer is precisely the same as the reason the majority of unintelligent people don't believe it. They don't want to because they're unwilling to accept the moral demands it would make on their lives. We can take a horse to water but we can't make him drink. A person must be willing to believe before he ever will believe. There isn't a thing you or I can do with a man who, despite all evidence to the contrary, insists that black is white.

We ourselves must be convinced about the truth we proclaim. Otherwise we won't be at all convincing to other people. We must be able to say confidently with Peter, ". . . we did not follow cleverly devised myths when we made known to you the power and coming of our Lord Jesus Christ" (II Peter 1:16). Then our witness will ring with authority, conviction, and the power of the Holy Spirit.

*The Christian doesn't commit intellectual suicide.*

# 6. Christ Is Relevant Today

**M**ANY people today are not so concerned with the question, Is Christianity true? They have a more practical question on their minds: Is it relevant? Student reaction is often: "So I believe what you've said about Jesus Christ—so what? What's it got to do with modern life? What's it got to do with *me?*" If we want to be effective in communicating the gospel of Jesus Christ to others, we need to know how it is relevant to us personally. Then we must consider how to relate the relevant realities of Jesus Christ, including events that occurred two thousand years ago, to life in the twentieth century.

Many people are today more open to spiritual realities than they were previously because of the climate of our times. Shortly before his death, the late Dr. Karl Compton warned that mankind faces annihilation unless the human race soon achieves moral and spiritual advances equivalent to its technological advances. *Life* magazine, in reporting the Nobel prize winners in physics several years ago, pointed out that the tremendously rapid advances in scientific understanding have been mere arithmetic gains in comparison to the geometric gains of ignorance. Each additional discovery multiplies man's realization of how much he does not know and cannot control. It also enables him to manipulate extensive new areas for ill as well as for good, e.g., nuclear energy which can be used to destroy cities or cancer. In spite of the fact that many attempt to extract morality from science, making science entirely amoral, metaphysical issues are more relevant and to the point today than ever before.

## Inner Emptiness

Many thoughtful people now realize that they cannot subsist on a diet of platitudes. How is the living Christ relevant to them? In considering present and eternal human needs, we find that the relevance of Jesus Christ to twentieth-century man is disclosed by His own words. The "I am" designations recorded in the gospel of John give us a clue as we see their relationship to modern man and his needs.

One basic need is for a filling of the spiritual vacuum, an answer to the inner emptiness that plagues many lives today. People often immerse themselves, in fact lose themselves, in all kinds of activity and external stimulation. But remove that external stimulation, get them alone with their thoughts, and they're bored, anxious, or miserable. They feel the aching void within and they can't escape it. They realize their lack of inner resources for the tests of life; all their props are external. Nothing external can produce lasting satisfaction. Satisfaction that lasts must come from what is inside us.

The Lord Jesus Christ says in John 6:35, "I am the bread of life; he who comes to me shall not hunger, and he who believes in me shall never thirst." A tremendous thing happens when we become personally related to Jesus Christ as a living Person. He enters our inner being and fills the spiritual vacuum as only He can. Because He is inside us through the indwelling presence of the Holy Spirit, we can have ultimate satisfaction. Augustine and many others throughout the centuries have echoed this discovery: "Thou hast made us for Thyself, O God, and our hearts are restless till they find their rest in Thee." God constructed us this way— creatures dependent on our Creator for completion and fulfillment. We can function as our Maker intended only when He is occupying the center of our lives.

Being released from dependence on external things for stimulation and pleasure in life is like sitting down to a sirloin steak after months of eating potato peelings. When we stop depending on outward and material things, we don't have to stop enjoying them. We can enjoy a concert, for instance, or the beauty of a sunset, to the glory of God. But we no longer depend on these things for our satisfaction in life. Like our Lord, we have meat to eat which others do not, namely doing the will of our Father in heaven (John 4:32). We draw from the resources that we have within us through the Lord Jesus Christ. We enjoy but do not depend on externals.

Jesus Christ is "the thing" many people are longing to get hold of. He is the One who will fill their aching void and free them from their false dependencies.

## Purposelessness

Another major area of need is the aimlessness, the purposelessness, that characterizes our age and the student world in particular. Many come up to me after a discussion and say, "You described me exactly. I don't know what I'm doing here in the university. I don't know why I'm eating three meals a day, studying architecture (physics, or whatever). I'm here because my folks are paying the bill, but I can't see what it's all about or what it's all leading to. I'm caught in a rat race of daily routines. It's hard to keep plugging away at the books when you can't see where you're going or why."

To this need the Lord Jesus Christ says, "I am the light of the world; he who follows me will not walk in darkness, but will have the light of life" (John 8:12). When we follow the Lord we discover purpose and direction in our lives, because we are living in the light of God Himself and of His will for us. We are no longer fumbling in the darkness of confusion. Have you ever groped about in a dark room trying to find the light switch? You brush against something. Then you feel something else trail across your face. You jump three feet and knock over a waste basket. Your heart skips a beat. You know this uncertain, insecure feeling. At last you find the light switch, turn it on, and orient yourself. Immediately you're secure. You know exactly how to proceed. Our experience is similar when we come to know the Lord Jesus Christ.

He leads us out of our confusion and uncertainty into His light. We see our lives in the context of God's will and purpose for history. That vision bestows significance, meaning, and purpose.

Most of God's will is already revealed for us in the Scripture. When we are obeying the will of God as we know it, He will make more of the details of His will clear to us. When we have told Him we're ready to accept His will whatever it may be, He gradually discloses to us those other details about where we should be and what we should do. These details, which mean so much to us individually, are in one sense quite incidental to the basic purpose of God. He is calling out for Himself a people from every tribe and tongue and people and nation, a people who will individually manifest the likeness of Christ. This is what God is doing in history. When He brings history to its conclusion, you and I will have the privilege of being part of God's eternal work.

Our lives have significance, meaning, and purpose not only for this life but for eternity. Think of it! Many people have some purpose in life at this moment. But most of these purposes are short-lived. They won't give ultimate satisfaction; they don't mean a thing in terms of eternity. To have ultimate meaning our lives must count not only for time, but also for eternity. We see so many people today who don't know what life is all about; they're groping around in darkness without Christ. They're as aimless as a ship without a rudder. If we relate the Lord Jesus Christ to them as the One who fulfills our need for direction and makes life purposeful, they may be attracted to Him and let Him meet their need.

## Fear of Death

A third need that the Lord Jesus Christ can meet is man's need for an antidote to the fear of death. When we're young death tends to be academic. We don't expect to die soon, so we don't give the possibility much thought. But death can rapidly become a prime consideration.

In this nuclear age an amazing number of young people have begun to think hard about death. They're keenly aware that we live on the brink of destruction. One push of a button and everything could be gone. The depth psychology polling of Samuel Lubell, who takes what people say and tries to deduce what they're actually thinking, revealed the key concern of American voters. For most, the latent issue in the presidential election was which candidate would best succeed in averting thermonuclear war. Although often kept beneath the surface, this threat of sudden destruction and death haunts the minds of men.

The Cuban crisis rattled the complacent as did the Berlin crisis before it. What will happen, they wondered, if the United States should get involved? I had just begun student work in 1950 when we were caught up in the Korean conflict. In every discussion with students someone would ask, "Suppose I'm shipped to Korea and a bullet comes up with my number on it. Where will I be after death? How can I be sure about life after death?"

The Lord Jesus Christ speaks with power to many whose minds are still troubled by death. In John 11:25, 26, He says, "I am the resurrection and the life; he who believes in me, though he die, yet shall he live, and whoever lives and believes in me shall never die." As we come to know Him in personal experience, Jesus Christ delivers us from the fear of death. Death ceases to be an unknown. We know it is simply the servant that ushers us into the presence of the living God whom we love. This knowledge enabled Paul to exult, "O death, where is thy victory? O death, where is thy sting?" (I Corinthians 15:55). Instead of fearing death, we anticipate the most dynamic experience we can ever have.

I hope none of us has succumbed to the naive impression of heavenly existence as sitting on pink cloud number nineteen and strumming a harp. Naturally, we'd all be terribly bored with heaven after the first week. Lest we fall for such silly thoughts, let's be assured that heaven will not be a boring place. We don't have all the details, because God hasn't chosen to give them to us; but from what He has told us we conclude that heaven will be a dynamic, expanding, creative experience far beyond anything our finite minds can now comprehend. It will be the essence of joy and satisfaction and song. Even though we don't fully understand what heaven will be, we look forward to being forever with the Lord. So we can suggest to others that Jesus Christ Himself is the solution to their present fears of death.

Until we ourselves face the prospect of death, however, we may not be sure experientially that Christ delivers us from this fear. It's wonderfully easy to say He does as you relax with friends around a warm fire after a scrumptious meal. It's quite different to say it when you're actually facing death. Situations such as impending surgery often brings an individual face to face with the fact of dying. When I underwent heart surgery ten years ago, I proved in the depths of my own experience Christ's power to conquer the fear of dying. This proof was a valuable by-product of the operation. Before I'd always maintained that Christians don't fear death, but I couldn't speak from personal experience.

When they came in to inject the anesthetic the morning of the operation, I was keenly aware of my chances. I knew that in all likelihood I would come back from the operating room, and yet there was a distinct possibility that I would never come back. A heart operation, you know, can be a complete success, but the patient may die because one of seventy-four other things has gone wrong. That morning a joy and peace that I knew came totally from outside of myself flooded my being. I'll never forget it. If I'd ever thought that peace in the face of death could be conjured up through the power of positive thinking, that idea was dispelled forever. I knew I didn't have it in me to face this crisis myself. Mortal fear had gripped the man across the hall who was going in for an appendectomy. If positive thinking could have done the trick, he could have talked himself out of his fear. As for me, strains of *The Messiah* pounded through my brain as I was rolled down the hall to the operating room. As the nurses dripped in the sodium pentothal, I could even joke with them about how long I would stay awake—I think I got to six before I lost consciousness. It was a wonderful experience for me to put this fact of reality to the test and prove it true. Because it is true, we can invite anyone who is seeking freedom from the fear of death to turn to the Lord Jesus Christ and find Him a relevant solution to their fear.

## Desire for Inner Peace

Another expression of need today is the longing for inner peace. A Christian doctor on the West Coast took an informal, three-year poll among his patients. He wanted to know what one wish each would make if he were assured that his wish would be granted. Peace of heart, mind, and soul was the number one desire of 87 per cent of his patients. The phenomenal sale of religious books in recent years also indicates this unmet need. People don't have inner peace but they want it desperately. Deep down they realize that everything in this life—material possessions, power, prestige, fame—will turn to dust and ashes. They yearn for the lasting inner peace and contentment that transcends these passing things.

Again our Lord supplies the answer to man's need. His promise in John 14:27 is more than sufficient: "Peace I leave with you; my peace I give to you; not as the world gives do I give to you. Let not your hearts be troubled." His peace differs from the peace the world gives. The peace we find in the world may seem real for the moment but then it's gone. "I am not of the world," our Lord said (John 17:14). Therefore He can give a peace that transcends this world, a peace that is deep-seated, permanent, eternal. This deep-seated peace of heart, mind, and soul grows out of our personal relationship of faith and dependence on the Lord Jesus Christ. He only asks us to accept His invitation, "Come to me, all who labor and are heavy-laden, and I will give you rest" (Matthew 11:28). People would pay millions of dollars if rest could be bought with money. But it's not available that way. The Lord Jesus Christ only gives His peace to those who will receive it as a free gift.

## Loneliness

Fifth, although we all have a basic need for love and security, loneliness is common today. A Harvard sociologist, David Riesman, emphasized this fact in his much-read book, *The Lonely Crowd*. He points out that many people are only existing as shells in the midst of a crowd.

Our Lord has dynamically related Himself to this particular need in saying, "I am the good shepherd. The good shepherd lays down his life for the sheep" (John 10:11). A shepherd looks after and cares for the sheep. Our Lord cared so much that He gave His life for His sheep. He has further assured us with the words, "Lo, I am with you always, to the close of the age" and "I will never fail you nor forsake you." A student from Barnard College of Columbia University came to see my wife one afternoon while we were living in New York City. She was utterly alone and felt she couldn't trust anyone because of past experiences with family and friends. As Marie told her about some of the ways Jesus Christ would meet the needs in her life, she looked up with tears in her eyes and asked, "Do you mean that He would never leave me; that He would always love me if I committed my life to Him?" My wife assured her that she meant just that, for the authority of our Lord's words and the proof of her own personal experience confirmed His faithfulness.

Has the presence of Jesus Christ ever dispelled your loneliness? Because I do a lot of traveling, I often find myself alone in Boondocks Junction, not knowing anyone. It's been wonderful at such times to claim the reality of the Lord's presence by faith and to recognize that I am never alone. It's tremendous knowing that we will never be alone because the Lord Jesus Christ is always with us. Sometimes when we imagine we're all alone we're tempted to do things that we wouldn't do if we remembered Christ's abiding presence with us. But when we consciously recognize and live in the light of His presence, we have a negative deterrent from sin as well as a positive dynamic for life.

## Lack of Self-Control

Many people face a problem of poor self-control: "I find myself doing things I never thought I'd indulge in. I vow I'm going to change, but I can't." When students open up about themselves, they almost always admit this problem. They've become involved in campus behavior that they would never have dreamed of back home. The maelstrom of social pressure sucks them in. Then try as they will, they can't escape its grasp. Our Lord speaks to this need by promising to give us life and power. In John 14:6 He says, "I am the way, and the truth, and the life." As we rely on Him, avoiding the temptations we would bring upon ourselves and trusting in His power to deliver us from the temptations that come unforseen, He releases His power in our lives and transforms our lack of self-control into deliverance from the power of sin. This transforming power characterizes the lives of many who have come to know Jesus Christ. It is especially evident in people who have been converted out of pagan backgrounds into a drastically different pattern of life. Jesus Christ has broken their chains of lack of self-control and given them power that they know couldn't come from themselves. This is one of the most potent relevancies of Jesus Christ to twentieth-century man.

## Thinking Needs Integration

In His words, "I am the way, and the truth, and the life," our Lord also speaks to another major need of man: integration in his thinking. A University of Wisconsin senior approached a Christian faculty friend of mine with this problem: "I've completed my 144 credit hours and in two weeks I'm going to graduate. But I feel like I'm leaving the university with a bagful of marbles in my hand. I don't see any relationships between the various courses I've studied. They don't seem to fit together. They're more like unrelated marbles in a bag." This fellow did not know Him who is the Truth—the One who is absolute truth, from whom all truth stems, in whom all truth is interrelated and tied together. All kinds of things begin to fall into place in Jesus Christ as we come to see Him as the One who ultimately is the only truth.

## Jesus Christ Is the Truth

We have authority as Christians to speak of Jesus Christ because He is the Truth. We don't communicate the gospel on mere pragmatic grounds, although the gospel is true pragmatically. Our approach does not present God as a cosmic bellboy who meets all our needs. We don't claim that Christianity is true because it works. No. Christianity works because it is true. Jesus Christ is the Truth. Our Lord spoke with devastating authority when He said, "Heaven and earth will pass away, but my words will not pass away" (Mark 13:31). And so we should not relate Jesus Christ to people simply from a pragmatic viewpoint, although it does represent one very *dynamic* aspect of the gospel. We must always base our communication on the revealed truth of God and the authority of Jesus Christ Himself. Then we can relate Jesus Christ to contemporary needs, showing the people around us that He can be relevant to them in personal experience. Our own personal experience of how Jesus Christ meets specific needs will help an individual to see how very relevant and reliable the promises of Jesus Christ are.

In this short chapter we certainly haven't covered all the needs of man in today's world, nor all the Lord's specific provisions for each of them. Neither are we pretending that once we receive Jesus Christ all our struggles are over. We do have problems in the Christian life, plenty of them. In fact, many Christians have more problems than ever before. The difference is that the Lord Jesus Christ is with us in the battle, and He makes all the difference in the world.

*Scratch where people itch.*

# 7. Worldliness: External Or Internal?

Genuine Christians want to live holy lives. James urged that we keep ourselves untarnished by the world (James 1:27). Paul repeated the Old Testament command, ". . . Come out from them, and be separate from them, says the Lord, and touch nothing unclean" (II Corinthians 6:17). Peter voiced God's requirement more positively, "You shall be holy, for I am holy" (I Peter 1:16). Today pastors and even well-meaning friends are apt to exhort us with these and similar verses.

But what do we mean by "spiritual" and by "worldly"? Before we can work toward genuine spirituality, we must have a definite and realistic understanding of these terms. Our ideas on the subject affect our treatment of young Christians converted from non-Christian backgrounds, the advice we give others for living holy lives, the methods we use with young children at Sunday School or at home. Our definition of holiness also influences our relationship with Christians who are more stringent, or more liberal, in their attitudes about various practices, amusements, and attitudes than we are.

Many people regard spirituality and worldliness as a list of do's and don'ts. Unintentionally, they debase the holiness God requires by making it a matter of rule-keeping.

The Bible is explicit in laying down the law about some areas of Christian behavior. For example, thou shalt not kill, thou shalt not commit adultery, thou shalt not steal, thou shalt not covet. Such commands are universal. They include all men in all places at all times, and they leave no room for doubt or difference of opinion. Anyone who prays for God's guidance to indulge in one of these activities is wasting his time; we can tell him so on the authority of God's Word.

Our disagreements about worldliness develop over other things that the Bible doesn't mention explicitly—radio, television, movies, dances, cards, cigarettes, cosmetics, *ad infinitum*. The list is endless because some group always blackballs another activity which restricts other Christians. Most of these taboos were unheard-of when the Bible was written, so naturally it is silent about them.

The absence of an explicit biblical standard for many of these debatable items is just the beginning of the problem. Geographical and cultural variations in the accepted "Christian standard" complicate the situation even more. During our three years in Texas it was very interesting to compare northern and southern behavioral standards. A good example is cosmetics. The use of beautifying aids raises no questions for the Texas Christian; she with her genuine, earnest faith uses them liberally. In the North where I grew up, on the other hand, many religious circles consider the use of lipstick as *prima facie* evidence that the "worldly" wearer can't possibly be in a vital relationship with Jesus Christ. Standards do vary.

When I visited the European continent I discovered that many French Christians drink wine as a matter of course. Their faith doesn't negate this accepted custom. Yet in many parts of the United States drinking has become a major issue. Sometimes people attach biblical authority to their own particular customs (customs which may be scripturally justified in their particular situation); then they generalize and attempt to legislate their own code of behavior for everyone. Behavioral patterns vary and the resulting diversity reflected at an international missionary candidates' school, for instance, is tremendous.

## What Is Legitimate?

The issue of legitimate Christian behavior is no new problem. In the first century Paul had to set both the Roman and Corinthian Christians straight on this matter. Speaking to the situation in Rome, Paul laid down basic principles in Romans 14. He addressed a cosmopolitan church that included Gentile believers—some who had never worshiped idols and others who had been converted out of pagan idolatry—as well as Jewish believers, who cherished a heritage of ceremonies and holy days. In Jesus Christ all these believers had been made one. But their backgrounds and behavior patterns caused differences nonetheless.

One controversy concerned meat. The disputed meat had probably been used in idol worship before being sold in the marketplace. We can assume that the Roman misunderstandings were similar to those at Corinth, described in I Corinthians 8:1-13 and 10:25-29. Some believers—probably the Jewish Christians—were eating this meat without any qualms. I can imagine one of them thinking as he entered the meat market, "It's been offered to a worthless idol? So what? Meat is meat and I like meat." You see, the Jews disclaimed any involvement in the meat's previous use. But other believers—old idol worshipers—were "real shook" because their brethren ate this meat. They had formerly eaten such meat as a part of their idol worship. In forsaking the idols they also forsook the meat; they didn't separate the two acts in their minds. So they were extremely upset to see a Christian buy and enjoy such meat.

A second controversy plagued the church at Rome. Probably it was the Jewish Christians this time who couldn't understand the Gentiles' scandalous disregard for holy days and feasts. The Gentiles, surprised that a little thing like this should disturb the Jews, probably asked, "What's that observance got to do with Christianity anyway? The crux of the matter is Jesus Christ. We've come to know Him. You can keep your holy days and feasts if you want them. That's fine with us; suit yourselves. But we can't regard them as inherent in Christianity."

There was tremendous tension on each score, and both groups made the same mistake—they assumed that their customs and culture were norms of Christianity. But the difficulty went deeper. People drew spiritual conclusions from a man's external behavior instead of seeking to understand his inner responses, his motivations. This subtle error catches us, too, if we're not careful. Since the Church of this century faces similar problems, let's consider Paul's relevant and applicable principles as he stated them in Romans 14.

### Don't Judge

We find the *first* principle in verses three and four, and again in verses ten through thirteen: "Let not him who eats despise him who abstains, and let not him who abstains pass judgment on him who eats; for God has welcomed him. Who are you to pass judgment on the servant of another? It is before his own master that he stands or falls. And he will be upheld, for the Master is able to make him stand." God is our Master and Judge. We are not entitled to set ourselves up as the judges of someone else. If the Scripture is not explicit about some activity, we have no right to criticize or condone another person because he behaves contrary to our opinions. This principle works in two ways. Let's apply it to a noncontroversial activity like putting together jig-saw puzzles. I may feel that I have the liberty to work on a puzzle. This liberty does not give me the right to call the person who refrains an "old fogey." On the other hand, perhaps I don't have the liberty to indulge in this pastime. I can't consequently accuse another Christian of being worldly because he sits down with a puzzle.

It's our attitude toward other Christians that counts here. Ninety percent of the tension over behavior would be eliminated if we could get our attitudes straightened out. Conformity isn't the solution. We don't need to adopt each other's behavior patterns. But we who are all so prone to judge need to accept each person and realize that he stands or falls before God—not us.

### Let Conviction Mold Behavior

The *second* principle, which appears in verse five, emphasizes our own responsibility before God: "One man esteems one day as better than another, while another man esteems all days alike. Let every one be fully convinced in his own mind." Personal conviction—not social pressure or some lesser motivation—should mold our behavior. As Christians we desire to honor the Lord Jesus Christ by doing whatever will please and glorify Him. And so we base our actions on what we believe to be the will of God for us. This tremendous internal principle will hold in every place and circumstance, every time.

We can see the meaning of this principle in connection with the training of a child. Because I now have two youngsters I'm very much aware of it. For example, if we try to clamp our son into a mold of do's and don'ts without helping him to understand the why's, he's apt to throw over all our prohibitions as soon as he escapes parental supervision. Why? Because he doesn't understand the principles involved. New Christians are children spiritually. We often try to make them conform to our accustomed behaviorisms before they've had a chance to discover personally God's will for them; then when they aren't with us, they usually abandon our whole behavioral system and revert to some of their preconversion ways. We need to be convinced that *our* behavior is to the glory of God. When we act or refrain from acting, with conviction for the Lord's sake, what we can and can't do is no longer a problem or burden, but a joy. As long as we are personally convinced in our own minds the principle will hold, regardless of situations and other people. But each of us needs to consider and reconsider his own behavior in the light of the New Testament to be sure he is following God's will for him.

### All of Life Is God's

The *third* principle points to the basis for our personal conviction. In verse eight we read, "If we live, we live to the Lord, and if we die, we die to the Lord; so then, whether we live or whether we die, we are the Lord's." The totality of our life is to be given over to God for His glory. All of our life—not just the moments we spend praying, reading the Bible, or witnessing, but the whole of our life—belongs to God. There are no separate compartments for the sacred and the secular in a Christian's life. You study the Bible to the glory of God. Your game of chess should be equally glorifying to Him. How can anyone play chess to the glory of God? It's simple if we first recognize that our whole life, every ounce of energy, every moment of time, every dime of money, and every other aspect belongs to Jesus Christ. We are simply His stewards, and He expects us to invest every part of our lives in terms of His will for us. There are times when I ought to be playing chess instead of studying the Bible. There are other times when I should be studying the Bible and not playing chess. We experience tremendous release from unnecessary tension as we realize this fact and live totally in the presence of God with the intent to honor Jesus Christ.

Sometimes Christians have trouble enjoying life. Did you ever have a guilty feeling because you enjoyed an oozing, drooling steak

that was just too delicious? There's no reason to feel guilty. In I
Timothy 6:17 Paul reminds Timothy of one of Scripture's great
facts, that it is "God who richly furnishes us_with everything to enjoy." Just because we áre Christians we can enter more fully than
others into every kind of enjoyment. The hymn puts it:

> Heav'n above is softer blue,
> Earth around is sweeter green!
> Something lives in ev'ry hue
> Christless eyes have never seen.

Instead of clinging to that vague uneasy feeling when we're finding
something pleasureful, let's enjoy all the things He gives us to the
glory of God.

"Is this what I should be doing right now?" That's the key
question to ask ourselves. Sometimes we need to be out shoveling
snow instead of praying; at other times we ought to forget the snow
and fall to our knees. Vital Christianity is not limited to the times
of so-called spiritual activity or the days or hours when we're involved in obvious Christian fellowship. Jesus Christ is as real and
dynamic at four o'clock Tuesday afternoon in the lab or library,
home or office as He is at eleven o'clock Sunday morning in
church. He enables us to go through the whole of life in His
presence, with Him right at our side. Every aspect, every moment
of our lives belongs to God and can glórify Him. Has this concept
ever burst through to you? Or do you cling to a compartmentalized
existence? Mentally sorting the things we do behind spiritual and
nonspiritual partitions may explain much of our failure to live a
zestful, through-and-through Christian life. As we grasp the concept that each moment can be lived in God's will for His glory, life
takes on a whole new dimension.

## Motivation Is God's Concern

The *fourth* principle appears in verse fourteen: "I know and
am persuaded in the Lord Jesus that nothing is unclean in itself;
but it is unclean for any one who thinks it unclean." Many things
are not wrong in themselves, but our use of them may be wrong.
We just mentioned steak. Food is necessary, but we can misuse
food and abuse our bodies through gluttony. Sex, a very wonderful
gift of God, becomes one of the most sordid things in life when its
function is distorted. In themselves these things are not wrong;
the wrong lies in their misuse. And so Paul is concerned with our

attitude toward things. If we believe it is wrong for us to indulge in a particular activity, but we do so anyway, we are guilty even if someone else thinks that particular action is right.

Involved in our attitude toward a thing is our concern for the "weak brother." Let's not regard a weak brother simply as a person who isn't strong enough to do what we feel at liberty to do. Nor as the domineering older Christian who wants to force his legalistic list of don'ts on everyone. Essentially the weak brother is a Christian who is immature in his thinking. Probably he's a young Christian who hasn't yet learned to distinguish between an act and the motivation behind it. Instead of asking the basic question, "Why should(n't) I do that?" the weak brother interprets spirituality in terms of external actions, probably taking his standards of evaluation wholesale from his family or church group.

God's concern, we must remember, is with our motivation. In Romans 14:6 Paul was really saying, "He who eats, eats to glorify the Lord; likewise, he who won't eat abstains to glorify the Lord." Here we have two extremes in behavior, but both are followed in honor of the Lord. A weak brother accepts one of these extremes as *the* right way to act and overlooks the motivation that makes it right. If he then sees someone following the other extreme, he'll be either offended or confused, or both. He needs to learn (and so do we sometimes) that the Christian's love for Jesus Christ and his desire to honor and glorify Him must always come first. Then what he does or doesn't do will follow.

So what do we do about weak brothers? Bowl them over and keep rolling? Some of the Roman Christians must have felt like saying, "Phooey on weak brothers anyway! They're just immature, so why bother?" Paul wasted no words in reprimanding them: "If your brother is being injured by what you eat, you are no longer walking in love" (verse 15). We, the supposedly mature Christians who realize the fallacy of basing spiritual judgments on external acts, must be mature enough to accommodate our brethren who still don't understand. Through the love of God we've got to refuse to stumble or throw a brother on any minor issue. In I Corinthians 8, 9, 10 (if this subject concerns you, meditate on 8:10-13, 9:19-23, and 10:23-33) Paul elaborates on our responsibility for weaker brothers. He himself had personally resolved, ". . . if food is a cause of my brother's falling, I will never eat meat, lest I cause my brother to fall" (I Corinthians 8:13). It's the kingdom of God, you see, not our personal liberty that's at stake. And the kingdom of God involves deeper matters than whether we keep a holy day, eat meat, or do the twentieth-century equivalent. Learn what this classic seventeenth verse of Romans 14 means, ". . . the kingdom of God does not mean food and drink but righteousness and peace and joy in the Holy Spirit."

When a deeper issue is at stake, we may need to accommodate ourselves to a weak brother so we can help him to realize what the Kingdom means. At the same time, we shouldn't let him get the idea that he can impose his pet behavior pattern on others. Our counsel may help him toward more mature thinking. This was Paul's purpose in writing to the Roman and Corinthian churches. He helped them to see beyond their immature emphasis on the external act and encouraged them to develop a more permissive and accepting spirit toward Christians whose behavior differed from their own.

I got some practical, first-hand experience with this problem at a student conference in New Jersey some years ago. There I met a fellow, a salesman, who literally worshiped baseball before he became a Christian. He would slave away all winter long so that he could be completely free for his god in the summer months. For something like twelve years he hadn't missed a single game in Philadelphia. He knew every batting average since 1910. He slept, ate, drank, and breathed baseball. Then he met the Savior and gave up his idol, leaving it at Jesus' feet.

Towards the end of our rugged and somewhat exhausting conference, this fellow overheard me suggest to another staff member, "Say, after the conference let's go over to Connie Mack Stadium and see the Phillies. They're playing the St. Louis Cards." The salesman was staggered. Incredulous, he stared at me and demanded, "How can you as a Christian go to a baseball game?" Now I've heard a lot of taboos in Christian circles, but this was the first time I'd heard baseball banned! I was flabbergasted and didn't know what to say. When he asked a second time, "How can you and Fred claim to be Christians and then go out to a ball game?" Fred and I started thinking and discussing the situation. As we talked to the salesman we uncovered his problem. Here was a man like the Gentile Christians in Rome, a former idol worshiper. Baseball had been a big thing to him; now he assumed that anybody who saw a game (ate meat), however removed from idolatrous intents, was worshiping baseball as an idol. Fred and I canceled our baseball date since our going would have needlessly disturbed our friend at a sensitive stage in his Christian life. But we also talked and counseled with him, and he gradually realized that not all Christians find baseball a problem. With his background, baseball will probably be a dangerous temptation to him for the rest of his life; this he knew. But later he also saw that he couldn't legislate for Christians who have no problem with the sport. It heartened us to see him begin to mature in his attitudes.

We have a responsibility for our weak brother. The biblical principle does not allow us to go along our way with a willy-nilly attitude, thinking "He's wrong, he's naive, he won't agree anyway, so I'll just ignore him." Nor does the biblical principle call us to conform to someone else's conscience apart from our own investigating and soul-searching. Instead, the biblical principle demands that we examine our motives: Am I doing this and not doing that because of love for Jesus Christ and a desire to honor and glorify Him? Or is the real reason a less universal one, a reason that won't hold if I move from one social or cultural group to another?

After our motive has been established, we still have to decide what our attitude toward some particular activity should be. This is especially a problem when the Scripture's position isn't explicit. I think we all realize by now that many secondary issues in Christian behavior fall into a gray area of relativism. What's right for you may be wrong for me. But Paul has some specific advice for us. In verses 14, 22, and 23 of Romans 14, he draws the line of distinction—doubt: "I know and am persuaded in the Lord Jesus that nothing is unclean in itself; but it is unclean for any one who thinks it unclean. . . . The faith that you have, keep between yourself and God; happy is he who has no reason to judge himself for what he approves. But he who has doubts is condemned, if he eats, because he does not act from faith; for whatever does not proceed from faith is sin." Once my salesman friend understood the situation, it would have been all right for me to take in the ball game as a recreational exercise. But it would still have been wrong for him to go, for in his case doubt and other moral issues were involved.

I've found this a very helpful rule of thumb: if there is any doubt about the propriety of some activity, hold off. But if conscience is clear before God and if the thing can be done to His glory, without confusing someone else in the process, do it with pleasure. Rejoice. Be happy about whatever God has given you to enjoy. This is Paul's clear-cut principle.

Someone, of course, will always misinterpret and abuse his privilege of personal liberty by taking it as license to do whatever he pleases. Such behavior negates everything Paul is saying here. I'm always suspicious of the one who flaunts his different behavior to show how "free" he is. He's missed Paul's tone and intent by a mile.

Love is the controlling factor of all that we do when we live the whole of our lives to the glory of God. After the marriage ceremony, no one tells his dearly beloved, "Well, now that the commitment's made and the ceremony's over, I'm going out and have a ball. See you later!" The love which draws two people together in the first place is the abiding basis of their marriage. When you love someone you want to do everything with and for that person that will please her (or him). It pains you most when something you've done brings displeasure or harm to her. Love constrains you. Augustine knew what he was saying in his classic statement, "Love God, and do as you please." And he wasn't suggesting compartmentalization. A "My sins are forgiven; now I can live like the devil" attitude offers *prima facie* evidence that a person does not know the love of his heavenly Father and crucified Savior.

An expression of love for the Lord Jesus Christ and a desire to live completely for His glory are evidence of the new life in Christ. When our personal liberty in Christ is directed by this motivation, it is a wonderful freedom—bringing glory to Christ, enjoyment to ourselves, and comfort and edification to others.

## Worldliness: Attitude of Self-Indulgence

In the final analysis, worldliness is essentially a self-indulgent attitude. It may take many forms but, more than the exterior series of behavior patterns, it is an internal attitude. The most common and the most subtle form of worldliness among Christians is probably pride. Some of the most worldly people abstain from doing all the things we usually call "worldly." They are worldly because their basic concern is themselves, their own comfort, their own prestige, their own material prosperity. Merely abstaining from certain things is no guarantee that we are spiritual.

Genuine spirituality is the viewing of everything from God's standpoint: considering and living every part of our life according to His standard of values and in terms of His revealed will for us, so that everything we say and do may bring glory to Jesus Christ who loves us and gave Himself for us.

*Worldliness is a state of mind.*

# 8. Faith Is The Key

**F**AITH is the key to maintaining the reality of our Christian experience. We accept the doctrine that we are saved by faith: through faith alone we come to Jesus Christ and invite Him into our lives as Lord and Savior. But we easily forget that faith must continue as the operative principle in our Christian lives from day to day.

## What Is Faith?

I wonder how many of us understand what faith is? Many non-Christian students automatically equate it with superstition. They think that in order to have faith they must kiss reason goodby. "I'm too intelligent to be taken in by 'faith' " they say. Non-Christians aren't the only ones who feel like that, though. Some Christians also equate faith with superstition. Deep down under they accept the Sunday School youngster's definition of faith: "It's believing something that you know isn't true." A lot of us, if we're honest about it, may feel the very same way. The good front we put up is only a facade. Underneath our sort-of faith we know that we don't really believe this or that statement. So our faith gets to be a real problem. We need to get several things straight about faith; then we'll be able to consider its practical role in our daily lives.

### Daily Experience

*First,* faith is a common occurrence. Many people mistakenly regard faith as a phenomenon reserved for emotionally disturbed people who can't make it in life without a crutch. Yet even those who think of faith as a prop or tranquilizer exercise faith every day of their lives. You've probably eaten at least one meal today that you didn't prepare yourself or see being prepared. As you ate, you had no way of knowing if that food contained poison, but you ate it none-theless—in faith. Perhaps it was blind faith; you may be suf-fering from food poisoning an hour from now. Probably though, you ate the meal because you had confidence in the one who cooked it, even though, as in a restaurant, the cook may have been unknown to you. You exercised reasonable faith. You also have faith in your academic institution and expect it to grant you a degree when you complete the prescribed courses. All scientific research and progress depends on faith, too. Although the objec-tivity of science and scientists is often stressed, their work rests on several unproved axioms which must be accepted—if you'll pardon the expression—by faith. For example, scientists must be-lieve there is an orderly reality to be observed, that causal laws apply to that reality, and that human logic is adequate to describe physical reality—even to understand the universe. Thus, faith is a genuine experience of everyone of us. The question we face is not, "Do we have faith or not?" but, "In what and to what extent do we have faith?"

### Validity of Faith

*Second,* faith is only as valid as the object (the person or thing) in which it is placed. Maybe you have implicit faith in your roommate. If he asks to borrow fifty dollars this afternoon, and you have fifty dollars, you'll give it to him. But suppose that, un-known to you, he's flunked out of school and is leaving town for good. All your faith and confidence in him won't bring back your money after he disappears tomorrow, never to return. Your faith in him can be only as valid as he is trustworthy.

Or we might think of a diseased little girl whose primitive father takes her through the jungle to the witch doctor. The father may have implicit faith in the concoction being brewed to cure her. But no matter how much he believes in the potion, his faith won't save his daughter's life if the brew is poison. Faith is no more valid than the object in which it is placed. His faith is no more than superstition.

This principle has a corollary: intense belief does not create truth. Faith's validity cannot be increased by intensity. We find a lot of naive thinking about this in the world today. People say, "Well I think it's just wonderful that you can believe that. It's true to you, even though to me it's not true." Believing doesn't make a wish true. The generalizations in which we trust may be pure superficialities. When a little old lady was robbed by a young man who had rented one of her rooms, she sadly said, "My but he was such a nice boy. He even had YMCA on his towels!" Although she still wanted to believe in his integrity, her belief couldn't create an objective truth. Belief does not create truth any more than failure to believe destroys truth.

Some years ago a man in Texas received word that he had inherited a large fortune from a relative in England. This Texan, a recluse living in poverty, had never heard of the English relative. Even though he was on the verge of starvation he wouldn't believe the news. His refusal to believe didn't change that fact that he was heir to a million dollars; instead, disbelief deprived him of enjoying the money. He died starving and poverty stricken. The objective truth remained, but he missed out on its benefits because he failed to claim them in faith.

In the realm of everyday human experience, we tend to treat facts as facts. Few of us have trouble accepting the concept that belief can't create, and disbelief can't destroy, objective facts. But when talking about God, many people are strangely naive. I've heard more than one student say, "Oh, I don't believe in God," as though that settled the question. And a friend will say "Heaven and hell? I can't believe that they're real places." Then he doesn't need to worry about them, he thinks; by disbelieving he has supposedly wiped them out of existence.

Dr. A. W. Tozer's distinction between faith and superstition may help us here. Faith sees the invisible but it does not see the nonexistent. As Hebrews 11:1 explains it, "Faith is the assurance of things hoped for, the conviction of things not seen." The eyes of faith see something that is real, although invisible. What superstition sees is unreal and nonexistent. As we learn to discern between unreality and invisible reality, we discover a world of difference between the two.

*To repeat: Everyone believes in something.* The object of his faith, not the intensity of his belief or disbelief, will determine his

faith's validity. Faith placed in something unreal is only superstition.

## Christ: The Object of Christian Faith

Since the object of the Christian's faith is the Lord Jesus
Christ, we must ask ourselves whether Jesus Christ is a valid object
for our faith. Many of us, after studying the facts, have concluded
that He is. Now, by putting the hypothesis to the test of personal
experience through a relationship with Him, we are proving His
absolute trustworthiness.

In salvation, we can't earn the forgiveness of sin or the gift
of eternal life. We receive them by faith. Faith alone, we realize,
brings us into our vital relationship with Jesus Christ. But later
we're apt to pull a switch in our thinking—an unconscious switch,
perhaps, but a devastating one. After starting the Christian life by
faith we try to live it by works. Although we admit that salvation
can't be earned by works, sometimes we imagine that we must
work out the Christian life by doing a certain series of things. This
idea is false. The same faith that introduces us to life in Jesus
Christ must continue to operate throughout our Christian life. The
object of our faith also continues the same: Jesus Christ the Lord.

Scripture points us clearly to Jesus as the constant object of
our faith. Writing in I Corinthians 1:30, Paul reminds us, "He
(God) is the source of your life in Christ Jesus, whom God made
our wisdom, our righteousness and sanctification and redemption."
Jesus Christ is to be our wisdom; He is our righteousness, sanctification, and redemption. Peter makes a more staggering statement
about our Lord in II Peter 1:3, "His divine power has granted to
us all things that pertain to life and godliness, through the knowledge of him (Jesus Christ) who called us to his own glory and
excellence." Catch this: In the knowledge of Jesus who has called
us by His grace, His divine power has already granted us all things
that pertain to life and godliness. Do you realize that because you
have received Jesus Christ into your life as Savior and Lord, right
now you have everything necessary for a life of godliness and holiness?

Most of us—I know I do—tend to ask God for little packages.
We'll say, "Lord I need more love;" or "I need more joy, Lord.
And I need more peace of mind, too." We need more of this and
more of that. But God doesn't supply us with a packet of love or

joy or peace. If He did, we would be foolish enough to think of them as our own achievements and go around boasting, "See how I love people. Just look at the power in my life. Don't overlook my peace of mind either." No, God knows better. He has given you and me everything we need in the Lord Jesus Christ. Once we've received Him into our lives and have established the personal relationship that's been mentioned so often in these chapters, we have all that God is going to give us. Absolutely everything that we need at this moment is in Jesus Christ—ours to appropriate, if we will. And Jesus Christ is living within us! As we lay hold of Him by faith each day, He will impart every necessary thing to us.

## Christian Experiences of Faith

But how does this theoretical statement become practical? How do we lay hold of our Lord by faith, and experience the reality of faith? By reality we mean that which is genuine and authentic, that which can be apprehended and relied on. We need to have such reality in our own lives; it's crucial for both our personal relationship with Jesus Christ and our approach to the world around us. How do we experience the genuineness of faith in Jesus Christ?

### What Is It?

To start with, we have to know what we're looking for. We've all run into the non-Christian who says, "I'd believe in God if you could prove Him to me." When we ask him, "What would you accept as proof?" he's staggered. He's never stopped to think about what he's looking for. He wouldn't recognize the evidence if he stumbled over it.

In our looking for genuineness in the Christian life, we may share his problem. We're a little hazy about what we're after. Are we waiting for someone else's experience—maybe a voice from heaven? A friend may have told us, "God spoke to me . . ." and we exclaimed, "That's tremendous!" But then we began thinking about ourselves: "God never speaks to me. I wonder why I've never heard voices. Maybe there's something wrong with me, something in my spiritual life, perhaps." It's easy to misunderstand another person's expressions. Then we get confused, and without knowing quite what we're looking for, we try to duplicate his experience. When we think we have to have a great ecstatic experience that will set us turning cartwheels or spinning like a top, our ideas about the reality of faith get all out of kilter. Soon we begin to get frustrated.

I don't hear an audible voice when God speaks to me. I hear His Word. Reading in your Bible morning after morning, do you ever sense that a particular passage is God's message to you for that day? Have you ever felt that God through His Word was saying something directly to you? That's an experience of reality. Have you ever known the peace of Jesus Christ in a crisis? That's reality. Can you find anything about your life that's different because Jesus Christ is in it? That difference is a reality of the Christian life. Stop a minute and ask yourself where you would be today if you had never encountered Jesus Christ. You may discover that there is more objective evidence of the work of Jesus Christ in your life than you'd thought.

By faith we know the reality of Jesus Christ. By faith we find Him more real to us than a close member of our own family. By faith we can "practice His presence"; that is, we can learn to think of Him as a Person who is continually present with us. Omnipresence, of course, is an attribute of God. It is a fact about God that Christians accept—but few act on. We can train ourselves to think of Him in concrete situations, to be conscious that He is with us *here* and *now,* to remember that His resources are always available to us. If we do so, we will find him an inexhaustible source of all we need.

### Temptations

Jesus Christ, Himself, is all we need. Suppose you're in a tense situation, tempted to blow your stack. You can't stand that roommate another minute. What do you do? This very moment you can turn to Jesus Christ in faith and say, "Lord, I can't love this clod. I don't have what it takes. Only Your love will do. Love him through me." Recognizing your lack, you come to Jesus Christ by faith at the moment of need.

For some of us the word *temptation* suggests only one thing: impurity. Impurity certainly is a temptation to reckon with, but all kinds of other things tempt us too, like the urge to backbite or slay with sarcasm. Christians seem to be susceptible to the sins of the spirit far more than to wrong external acts. We can afford to be less concerned about the many external temptations that don't bother us, but we need to be more alert for the internal temptations that come up all the time. The Lord is waiting to hear us pray, "Lord, I need your patience for I'm impatient. The pressures are getting me down, and I don't have it in me to fight them. Thank you that you live in me, and that you're willing to release your patience. Please do so in my life now."

Temptations in the thought life must be nailed at the outset. You've heard this old adage, I'm sure, but it bears repetition: you can't stop the birds from flying over your head, but you can keep them from building a nest in your hair. Just as soon as we're tempted with an unclean thought, or an unjust or malicious one, we need to turn to Jesus Christ and say, "Lord, I don't have the power to beat this thing. Inside me is a wretched response to evil. But you do have the power. I'm turning to you to release your power in my life." Instead of looking to Jesus for victory, some of us have tried to battle the temptation ourselves. This is what defeats us. Suppose I say, "Don't think about white elephants for the next five minutes." Try as you will, you'll never succeed. Inherent in trying not to think about white elephants is a concentration on them.

We need to look past the tempting situation and see Jesus. "Lord, you are the source of love. I can't love this person (I almost despise him); but you do. Help me." Jesus Christ is all we need. Instead of more packages of love, peace, purity, or power, He offers us Himself, a living Person. What do we honestly think of His offer? What is Jesus Christ to us? To you, is He simply a series of facts on a piece of paper; or is He, right now, a living Person? If Jesus Christ doesn't seem alive—He is, whether we realize it or not—if you don't realize that He's living within you by the Holy Spirit and that He wants to commune with you, then He's obviously going to be meaningless to you. To have the truth that the Lord Jesus is a living Person burst upon you anew is a revolutionary experience. The life of faith day by day is just a continuing recognition of the risen, living Lord.

## Focus Attention on Christ

We're faked out sometimes because we spend too much time worrying about whether our faith is strong enough. Satan has us working from the wrong end of the stick. Hudson Taylor had to learn this truth and so do we. He described his (and our) plight in one of his letters: "All the time I felt assured that there was in Christ all I needed, but the practical question was—how to get it *out* . . . I saw that faith was the only requisite . . . but I had not this faith."[1] One day in China he received a letter from a friend which pointed out the solution: "But how to get faith strengthened? Not by striving after faith, but by resting on the Faithful one,"[2] "by looking off to the Faithful One."[3] Not faith itself, but the Object of our faith requires our attention. We should never be absorbed with our faith, disregarding the Object that determines it. Look to Jesus Christ. Someone has said that strong faith in a weak plank will land you in the river, but weak faith in a strong plank will get you across.

Faith lays hold of the "givens" in the Christian life and lives in the light of them. It's not always easy to do. Depression hits; you feel miserable. How can you get out of the dumps? Not by dwelling on your depression and all the things that have gone wrong. Sit down and ponder instead the amazing facts about Jesus Christ: who He is, what He has done in history, what He has done in your own life. Think of Him now, as the great High Priest, appearing in the presence of God for 'you—compassionate, able to save you to the uttermost. Allow yourself to meditate about Him for ten or fifteen minutes and involuntarily you'll find yourself singing.

Daily personal fellowship with the Living God is vitally important. When we haven't been alone in the presence of God for a while, we have trouble thinking of anything except the problems bugging us. Try this now. Meditate on what God has done in Jesus Christ and how He is God's gift to you. You'll find Him lifting you out of yourself. The prayers of the Bible follow this basic pattern: men remind themselves of who God is and of all He has done and then they pray about their own situation. They may start with creation and then recall what God did with Israel or Elijah. After gaining momentum and confidence they pray, "Now Lord, here we are. Give us courage and wisdom for the present situation."

---

1 Mrs. Howard Taylor, *Hudson Taylor's Spiritual Secret* (Chicago, Moody Press, 1955), p. 160. I commend this short biography of the founder of the China Inland Mission to you for your reading and rereading.
2 Ibid., p. 161.
3 Ibid., p. 156.

We need to be reminded of God's mercies in our own lives. Christians have short memories when it comes to their experiences with God. Reminding ourselves of what God has done in the past increases our confidence in the face of present problems. I believe such concrete reminders of God's love, wisdom, and power are the shield of faith which Paul in Ephesians 6:16 exhorts us to take to quench all the flaming darts of the evil one. What are his darts? Certainly they include the temptations of doubt and nervousness as we think about the unknown path which lies ahead.

## God's in Charge

Faith recognizes the fact that God is in control of my life. Whether I believe it or not, it's a fact that God is in control of the world. If I don't believe it, I'm just robbing myself of the enjoyment of the fact. But if I meditate on this fact and lay hold of it, my fears about the future vanish.

Experience proves this. A lot of my traveling from campus to campus is by air. Just before I'm scheduled to fly somewhere, my wife usually hears about several recent plane crashes. Such news never reassures us. In fact, I would probably cancel my flight if I didn't have the confidence that my life is in God's hand, that my family is also in His hand, and that nothing will happen in our lives by accident. Some men who have no assurance about their future really sweat it out during a plane flight. I don't. You see, a man has faith in God's care or he doesn't. The statement that God *is* in control is either true or it's not true. If it's not true we'd better forget about God. But if it is true and we accept God's revelation of Himself, our faith enables us to enjoy and rest in the certainty of His providence.

Faith gives our lives an amazingly new perspective. Faith acknowledges God's sovereign control but is not fatalistic. Fatalism submits to a blind, impersonal force over which man has no control. Faith in the providence of God yields willingly to a loving heavenly Father, who sees the two sparrows that fall to the ground and who numbers the hairs of each head. Faith is a far cry from fatalism and in that difference there is great comfort.

Faith encounters many challenges. Dr. Edward Carnell likens the Christian to a physicist watching a magic show. Each successful trick threatens the physicist's faith in the law of uniformity. He may admittedly be baffled, but his faith is not overthrown because the law of uniformity depends on scientific rather than private grounds. Similarly, the Christian's faith is strengthened as he keeps the promises of God before him and considers, not "the difficulties in the way of the things promised, but the character and resources of God who has made the promise."[4] Job did just this in response to his wife's taunts when God seemed to have abandoned him to incredible suffering. "Don't be an idiot. Curse God and die!" But Job declared, "Though he slay me, yet will I trust Him."

Habakkuk was bewildered by the events of his day. Judah lay in moral ruin, but God wasn't judging the people. When the prophet asked, "How come?" the Lord answered him, "I'm going to use Chaldea to chastise them." Habakkuk found it even harder to swallow that explanation for Chaldea was more wicked than Judah. Habakkuk had to learn to take the long view of God in His dealings with men. Only then could he confidently affirm, "Though there be no external manifestation of Thy presence and power, O God, I will trust in Thee. Though there be no figs on the tree, no cattle in the stalls, yet will I joy in the Lord and praise the God of my salvation" (Habakkuk 3:17, 18). We see faith here, not wishful thinking. Faith recognizes the realities that have now been revealed in the Lord Jesus Christ; faith takes hold of them and lives in their light.

### Faith in Daily Life

Genuine living by faith is a day-by-day experience. Yesterday's leftover manna cannot satisfy us today. We must continue in God's presence every day. There's no debate about this. It is a simple, but profound fact—and a crucial one in our life with God.

Perhaps you've heard of George Mueller, the founder of orphanages in England, who as a man of faith never made a public announcement of his needs but depended on God to provide for every necessity. George Mueller taught me a valuable and a comforting lesson about our daily fellowship with God. You see, I used to have the idea that once a Christian had it, whatever "it" was, all his problems would be ended. He'd always see the beaming sunlight, hear the birds twittering, and feel like turning cartwheels for joy. But even George Mueller admitted, "I consider it my greatest need before God and man to get my soul happy before the

---

[4] Edward J. Carnell, *The Case for Orthodox Theology* (Philadelphia, Westminster Press).

Lord each day before I see anybody." The key word is *get*. His soul wasn't always happy when he woke up. He must have felt just like I do when the alarm clock sounds. You know that cold-mashed-potatoes feeling that comes when you wake up and begin to remember all your problems? I'm sure he knew this feeling. As the day's first task, Mueller got himself into the presence of God to meditate on Him until his soul became happy in the Lord. Then he faced the day.

The Christian life isn't an entirely passive affair. I prefer a description like "victorious battle" to "victorious life" because the latter is apt to leave the false impression that Christians have no problems. There are struggles. My reading of the New Testament and my own experience have confirmed this. Life is a battle, but it is a victorious battle when by faith we daily lay hold of the realities of Jesus Christ and let Him be active in our life.

I think that sometimes we've made the "victorious Christian life," or "being filled with the Holy Spirit," or whatever you want to call it, far more complicated than it is. Some people may call me naive, but I've read every conceivable book I can find on the subject and I've talked to people about it by the hundreds. I've heard plenty of formulas. As I've read the New Testament and talked to others, I've concluded—and I'm open to correction—that, call it what you will, the key is being totally sold out, without reservation, to Jesus Christ.

The reality of such faith carries us through all life's vicissitudes. Sometimes we feel emotional about our Lord, at other times not. This is healthy. No one could last long at a high fever pitch of emotion; he'd wear out. Imagine what it would be like to constantly live at the emotional level you hit during the last seconds of a tied (your team has the ball) championship basketball game. We have our moments of intense emotion, but then our feelings undulate. But whether we feel emotionally high, low, or just pretty level-headed, underneath we can know the reality of Jesus Christ and His gift of pervading peace and contentment.

Knowing Jesus Christ we're no longer tied to circumstances. We don't bob up and down at their command. Instead, we're tied to the living and unchanging God. We can step over circumstances as we day by day walk with Him through faith, actively receiving His life and allowing Him to work it out in us. Because of His life, Paul was able to sing in prison. Don't kid yourself about Paul. He didn't get a boot out of living in prison or receiving thirty-nine lashes. Such hardships were as devastating for him as they would be for us. In Jesus Christ, though, he had found what enabled him to transcend his circumstances. Depending on the life of Christ in him, Paul's life was a genuine experience of faith.

A hymn that expresses well the reality of living by faith in all the varieties of life is based on the promise of Jesus' continuing presence. He said, "I will never fail you nor forsake you" (Hebrews 13:5); "Lo, I am with you always, to the close of the age" (Matthew 28:20). As we lay hold of this basic promise and live in its light, we can share in the genuine life of faith which this writer affirms:

> *I take Thy promise, Lord, in all its length,*
> *And breadth and fulness, as my daily strength,*
> *Into life's future fearless I may gaze,*
> *For, Jesus, Thou art with me all the days.*
>
> *There may be days of darkness and distress,*
> *When sin has pow'r to tempt, and care to press*
> *Yet in the darkest day I will not fear,*
> *For, 'mid the shadows, Thou wilt still be near.*
>
> *Days there may be of joy, and deep delight,*
> *When earth seems fairest, and her skies most bright;*
> *Then draw me closer to Thee, lest I rest*
> *Elsewhere, my Saviour, than upon Thy breast.*
>
> *And all the other days that make my life,*
> *Mark'd by no special joy or grief or strife,*
> *Days fill'd with quiet duties, trivial care,*
> *Burdens too small for other hearts to share. . .*
>
> *Spend Thou these days with me, all shall be Thine*
> *So shall the darkest hour with glory shine.*
> *Then when these earthly years have pass'd away,*
> *Let me be with Thee in the perfect day.*[5]

---

[5] H. L. R. Deck, "I Take Thy Promise, Lord", *Hymns*, Paul Beckwith, ed. (Chicago, Inter-Varsity Press, 1947), p. 6.

*It does matter what you believe as long as you believe it.*

# 9. Feeding The Spring

CHARACTER, someone has said, is what you do when nobody sees you. But most of us are more concerned with what others see. We concentrate on what we say and do in a social situation, the kind of impression we want to leave; we don't worry about our thoughts and actions when we're alone. Yet it's then that our true character comes out. We "let our hair down" and put our feet up on the table. We're really ourselves.

In his helpful and penetrating book, *The Meaning of Persons,* Dr. Paul Tournier comments on the disparity between what we are inside and what we appear to be to other people. He calls this disparity the difference between the person and the personage. Under most circumstances our degree of mental health will be greater if what we appear to be closely approaches what we actually are. The further apart our person and our personage are, the greater will be our problem in mental health, for a part of our lives will be a lie.

## The Secret Self

Throughout the Scripture God has emphasized that our real self is the person, the inner or secret self, the character that shows up when we're all alone. And God knows everything about our inner self. He reminded Samuel of the significance of the inner life when He sent him to anoint a son of Jesse as king. Samuel thought that tall, handsome Eliab had everything until the Lord told him, "Do not look on his appearance or on the height of his stature, because I have rejected him; for the Lord sees not as man sees; man looks on the outward appearance, but the Lord looks on the heart" (I Samuel 16:7). The heart, our inner life—that center of our personality that includes intellect, emotion, and will—is the basis for God's evaluation of us. And the writer to the Hebrews affirms His knowledge of all the facts: ". . . before him no creature is hidden, but all are open and laid bare to the eyes of him with whom we have to do" (Hebrews 4:13).

These are some of the most encouraging and the most frightening words in the Bible. They assure us that God always understands. Our very best friend will sometimes misunderstand. Often unintentionally, he may misinterpret a word or motive, and sadness follows. But God knows the whole truth. We can confide in Him because He knows us through and through. This very fact means, though, that we can't put up a front with Him. At times it's frightening to realize that He knows everything I know about myself, and more than I know. The living God sees me as I am when I'm all alone—stripped of all pretense.

We should consider our secret life, which no one but God sees, from both a negative and a positive perspective. Moses speaks of the negative aspect in Psalm 90:8, "Thou hast set our iniquities before thee, our secret sins in the light of thy countenance." This statement reveals several important facts.

*First, we all have secret sins.* Moses specifically says *our* iniquities, *our* secret sins. He excludes no one. Our secret sin may be hidden pride which through self-inflation makes a person see himself as better, smarter, kinder, more attractive and important than he is. It may be self-deception which encourages us to rationalize our behavior so that we have "justifiable gripes," "understandable frustration," "righteous indignation." It may be dishonesty which conceals half the truth or intentionally acts or speaks to create a false impression. It can be selfish hurry, careless waste of time or talents, or failure to love as God loves us. It may be wanting anyone or anything outside of God's will for us. It may be bitterness or animosity toward a particular person or group of people that is eating us, destroying us as the worm bored through Jonah's gourd. It may be cheating. It may be impurity. But whatever it is, God knows all about it. We can't hide it from Him. Instead, in His presence we need to acknowledge and come to grips with our hidden sin.

*Second, secret sin eventually leads to outward sin.* Open sins are the fruits which grow from the root of secret sin, often sins of motive. That frightens me. Our Lord dealt with this critical condition when He tried to explain to the Pharisees that sin is not necessarily external. Essentially, He said, "You don't understand. It's not what goes into a man that defiles him; it's not what people see him doing or not doing. It's from within, out of the heart of man, that evil thoughts, impurities, and all these other things come. Man is defiled from within" (c.f. Mark 7:14-23).

Secret sin known only to us always precedes outward sin which is apparent to others. James makes this point: " . . . each person is tempted when he is lured and enticed by his own desire. Then desire when it has conceived gives birth to sin; and sin when it is full-grown brings forth death" (James 1:14-15). Throughout the Bible we find examples: Achan's theft was preceded by a greedy heart. David's adultery began in his imagination. Ananias and Sapphira were only revealing their inner deceit when they lied to God. In each instance the sin existed within the person long before an external deed manifested it.

Perhaps we make a cutting remark about someone—that's outward; but an uncleansed disposition lies behind it. Whatever sin we may mention can be traced back to a faulty inner attitude, a secret sin. This fact helps us understand the statement that collapse in Christian life is never a blowout. It is always a slow leak. I wonder if there are any slow leaks in my life or yours right now.

*Third, we must realize that all our secret sins are before God.* If we have any He sees them, even though we may not be aware of them. If we are personally unaware of sin, we can open our hearts and minds to God and ask Him to show us whether there is secret sin in our lives, depending upon Him to answer. As we honestly pray with David, "Search me, O God, and know my heart! Try me and know my thoughts! And see if there be any wicked way in me, and lead me in the way everlasting" (Psalm 139:23-24), the Holy Spirit will convict us of sin in our lives. He may reveal it to us through a passage of Scripture we're meditating on or He may use someone else's remark to trigger our awareness of it. One way or another, He will put His finger on the sin.

It's up to us to come to grips with that particular sin, once it's been revealed. God never reveals sin to us to leave us in it. Even while He is awakening our awareness of it, He offers forgiveness and cleansing. He wants us to respond to His revelation by confessing and forsaking that particular sin and by making restitution if it is necessary. He wants to forgive and cleanse us. He wants to remove that secret sin from us. He wants to empower us to live for Him. And so He is always ready to hear our request for forgiveness, cleansing, and power.

Satan, who doesn't want us to deal with newly discovered sin or repeated sin in our lives, delights in taunting us with the suggestion, "Not again! You don't have the gall to go back to God and confess this same sin again, do you? You just finished confessing that sin the other day and you promised the Lord that you'd forsake it. How can you face Him now? You'd better improve your batting average first. Show Him that you've got the will power to lick it once and for all." These words come from the Pit. God wants us to come to Him immediately, just as we are. Only He can deal with us and our sins. He knew exactly what we were like when He redeemed us in Jesus Christ on the cross. As the illuminating work of the Holy Spirit makes our sin apparent to us, He calls us to come just as we are—without one plea except the blood which the Lord Jesus shed for us.

If the Holy Spirit doesn't reveal any specific sin in our lives after we have asked Him to, we don't need to agitate ourselves. One of the enemy's devices to paralyze us and prevent our effectively serving Jesus Christ is to suggest that we are guilty of some unknown sin which God hasn't revealed to us. Satan hopes that instead of resting in His peace and rejoicing in past and present cleansing and forgiveness we'll grow introspective. If we become absorbed with ourselves we'll tend to forget others. Our Father wants us to recognize that our capacity for sin, and for self-deception concerning sin, is virtually limitless. Jeremiah the Prophet pointed out that the heart is deceitful above all things and desperately wicked (Jeremiah 17:9). Yet we are to rely on the Savior who keeps on saving and who takes the responsibility for revealing specific sins to us. Thus He relieves us of anxiety and constant self-concern. We can focus our minds on the Lord Jesus Christ, the solution for every sin problem, with a kind of carefree relaxed trust that should characterize the child of God.

Robert Murray McCheyne struck a good balance when he

advised, "For every look you take at yourself, take ten at Jesus Christ." We don't want to be morbidly introspective, like people who take their spiritual temperature every three days or every three hours. Often we treat our spiritual life like the little boy who planted a lima bean, then dug it up every morning to see how it was growing. It is through committing every area of our lives to Him and then in trusting Him that we grow in the personal fellowship with God for which we were intended.

## Guard and Develop Your Inner Life

Because of the impact which our inner life has in determining our outward life, the Scripture explicitly admonishes us to guard that inner life: "Keep your heart with all vigilance; for from it flow the springs of life" (Proverbs 4:23). We are in large part determined by our inner life. Someone has observed that circumstances never make or break anyone; they simply reveal him. We are a day-by-day accumulation of everything that has constituted our life until this point in time—especially of what we have thought, felt, and willed.

This is why the psalmist says, "Behold, thou desirest truth in the inward being: therefore teach me wisdom in my secret heart" (Psalm 51:6). Here we move from the negative to the positive aspect of our secret life, personal fellowship with God Himself. In James 4:8 we read, "Draw near to God and he will draw near to you. Cleanse your hands, you sinners, and purify your hearts, you men of double mind." Although ultimately we depend on God alone to redeem and cleanse us, He gives us a positive, active role to take in the process.

This positive aspect of our inner life may and should be even more influential than the negative in determining our external life. Later in the Sermon on the Mount, Jesus taught, ". . . when you pray, go into your room and shut the door and pray to your Father who is in secret; and your Father who sees in secret will reward you" (Matthew 6:6). Secret prayer will receive an evident reward from the Father. Our secret life with God is the root of outward spiritual power, just as secret sin is the root of outward sin. Both are inexorable spiritual laws.

Incredible as it is, the God of creation, who made heaven and earth and us, wants to have personal fellowship with each one of us. What a tremendous fact to lay hold of! We can scarcely grasp its import. Throughout Scripture we see evidence of men in this intimate relationship with the Lord. David affirmed, "O Lord, in the morning thou dost hear my voice" (Psalm 5:3). Three times a day Daniel bowed down toward Jerusalem to commune with the living God, and then he faced the consequences—lions. After a long and busy day, our Lord rose before daybreak and went out to a lonely place to be alone with His Father.

God enjoys the worship, praise, and fellowship of a group of believers gathered in the name of Christ. He is pleased to meet us in chapel, church, and student prayer meetings. But He also likes to meet us alone. Suppose your parents never saw you except when you brought a crowd of friends home. Like most parents, they would probably be glad to meet your friends. They want to share your interests. But wouldn't they also become frustrated if this were the only context in which they saw you? They might say, "Look, we like your friends but we want to see you alone for a while. How about an hour with no one but you?" This is just the way God must feel about some of us. Of course we spend time with Him in certain groups, yet He longs to meet us as individuals.

Now suppose that you wanted to give your parents a special gift. To buy it you had to spend all your time working; you never got home. How would they feel? When they couldn't stand it any longer, wouldn't they burst out, "Look, we don't want your gift; we want you! We'd like a little time with you." It is easy to get so involved "serving the Lord" that we never have any time to spend alone with Him. Yet it is those hours alone with Him that are essential to a life that possesses spiritual power.

What happens when we meet with God alone? What is necessary if that secret time with the living God is to result in manifest spiritual power? He, of course, speaks to us through His Word, and we respond to Him in prayer. Yet sometimes our Bible reading or praying leaves us unsatisfied. What goes wrong?

### Bible Study

In studying the Bible many people seek to discover facts about the Bible, even facts within the Bible. But information about the written Word is not an end in itself. If you've ever tried to produce spiritual life and power simply by reading verses, organizing information, and making outlines, you know it's a futile effort. Benjamin Franklin wrote commentaries on the Bible, but as far as we know he never became a Christian.

Basically, the Bible's purpose is to bring us into contact with the living God in Jesus Christ; as one hymn writer put it, *"Beyond the sacred page we seek Thee, Lord."* A telescope helps to point us to the star. Of course we should know how the telescope works to use it, but what a tragedy when we get engrossed in its operation and forget to look for the star. Failure to distinguish between the means and the end may be the problem a lot of us have in our personal devotions or "quiet time." Maybe we're thinking, "I've tried a regular quiet time, but it was dry as dust. I couldn't get anything out of it." Have you ever felt as though you were cranking out ten verses a day, like a Buddhist spinning his prayer wheel, and it didn't mean a thing to you? You began to feel discouraged: What's the use, why bother? Very similar feelings hit most of us at times. There's no sense in acting out empty ritual. Maybe we've failed to recognize that the purpose of our quiet time is to come face to face with the living God Himself, in the Lord Jesus Christ. Or maybe we've failed to realize that He is a living Person who wants to meet us. We should always come to the Scripture expecting to meet the living Lord, for essentially His Word is not a textbook but a revelation of Himself.

Another problem we may experience in our personal Bible study arises from lack of direction. It's been said, "He who aims at nothing is sure to hit it." If we enter our quiet time with no sense of purpose, no felt desire for personal fellowship with the Lord Jesus Christ, this fact will stunt the growth of our spiritual life as surely as loss of appetite will depress our physical life.

Seven directive questions have helped me immensely as I've used them from time to time in my own Bible reading. I tried them when I was just beginning to meet with God every morning, and I still refer to them occasionally, especially if the approach I'm currently using starts to go stale on me. If you come to the Word of God prayerfully and search the passage for answers to each question, you'll discover pertinent applications every time. A few of the seven questions may not fit a particular passage but others will. Some apply to every passage. Although simple, these questions can keep us from whizzing through a string of verses with our mind on today's schedule or yesterday's events. They arrest our flights of thought and bring us face to face with the living God and His will.

*First: Is there an example for me to follow?* Does this passage of Scripture suggest anything that I should do or be today? Instead of reading Scripture as an academic exercise, we should always consider God's truth with the intent to pattern our lives according to His revealed will. What example is there for me to follow?

*Second: Is there a sin for me to avoid?*

*Third: Is there a command for me to obey?* We often wonder about God's will for our lives. And we often talk as though discerning God's will for us were a difficult and perplexing problem.

Do you realize that ninety-five percent of His will has already been revealed? This can be a shattering discovery. God has revealed His will in the Bible. In our long impressive prayers about seeking the will of God we're usually thinking in terms of marriage or a career. But from one point of view these two decisions are incidental. God clearly states His will for our character and daily life. Sometimes we don't know His will for one reason only: we haven't exposed ourselves to the Word of God to look for it.

Is there a command to obey? If—as so often happens—we have been disobedient about something God has made clear, we can't expect Him to disclose more of His will to us. First He expects us to obey what He has shown us, for His declared will is not optional to us. God reveals His will to us progressively, according to our obedience.

*Fourth: Is there a promise for me to claim?* In this passage of Scripture is the Holy Spirit directing me to a promise which I can now possess by faith? Some promises in Scripture, like Hebrews 13:5, are unconditional: "I will never leave thee, nor forsake thee." Others have a condition attached to them, "Delight thyself also in the Lord; and he shall give thee the desires of thine heart" (Psalm 37:4). As we search for the promises, we need to see and think through their conditions too, and then claim them accordingly.

*Fifth: What does this particular passage teach me about God, or about Jesus Christ?* The adventure of Christian life in many ways resembles marriage. No engaged couple really know each other. Although each has tried to discover as much as possible about the prospective partner, by their first wedding anniversary they'll look back and realize, "I didn't know her (or him) when I married her, and she (or he) didn't know me." This parenthetically, is reason enough for me to shudder at the thought of any marriage that lacks the certainty of God's will. You don't really know the other person beforehand. The process of getting to know one's partner is one of the great adventures of marriage.

Similarly, one of the adventures of the Christian life is growing in our personal knowledge of the Lord Jesus Christ. At the outset we know a few things about Him, enough to commit our lives to Him and receive Him into our lives as Lord and Savior. We trust Him. We commit our lives to Him in total obedience. Yet we scarcely know Him. By meditating on His own revelation of Himself and by growing in Him, we get to know God better and better. Then as life goes on, through our own personal experiences with Him, He gives added dimensions to a fact we have already learned about Him in the Scripture; e.g., that God is merciful, that God honors His word.

*Sixth: Is there a difficulty here for me to explore?* Some people always look for the questions first, only to get swamped by problems and difficulties. Before long they alibi, "There are so many things I don't understand. I can't make head or tail out of them; it's no use even to try." When we eat fish, most of us set aside the bones so we can eat the fish itself. But a few major on the bones and never get to the fish. Whether eating fish or studying the Bible, bone-picking does not satisfy. We should jot down questions that puzzle us, then look for their answers later. But we shouldn't make the problems the main course of our meal.

*Seventh: Is there something in this passage that I should pray about today?* Some of us have trouble with prayer. Every day seems the same—nothing more than a repetition of yesterday's words, "O Lord, bless me and Mom and Mary and the whole world, for Jesus' sake, Amen." If we're alert as we read through the Scripture, we can draw our prayer from the passage at hand. The freshness of such prayer helps us discover the joy of a full-orbed prayer life based on Scripture itself.

Not all passages contain an example to follow, a sin to avoid, a command to obey, a promise to claim, a new thought about God, a difficulty to explore, and a matter for prayer, but each includes some of these. If you'll take fifteen minutes tomorrow morning, or even today, to meet with God and look for answers to these questions in some passage of Scripture, I guarantee you a rewarding search.

The next problem is what to *read for a balanced spiritual diet.* Perhaps, like many other Christians, you tend to range among the

23rd Psalm, the gospel of John, and a few other favorite passages. Fearing the unfamiliar, you let the rest of the Bible go by default. Yet as Christians who must come to grips with the whole counsel of God, we need a planned system for reading through the whole Bible. This is the goal of *Search the Scriptures* and *This Morning with God* and also of Scripture Union's worldwide fellowship of Bible readers. Whether we follow someone else's system or devise our own, it is essential that we follow some plan.

*Wandering thoughts* and other distractions may also plague us. That physics exam or the ball game or some coming event proves so absorbing we can't concentrate. Keep pencil and paper handy to write down new facts and ideas met in reading as one of the best cures for this problem. Notes taken in our quiet time become a record of fresh, first-hand discoveries with God. Incidentally, these faithfully kept notes may be a lifesaver if, unexpectedly, we're called on to give a 15-minute devotional message. Further, our words will have the warmth and power of genuine experience as we relate a recent discovery made in personal fellowship with God.

We need to be reminded that *we can't evaluate our quiet time by the way we feel* afterwards. Some days an idea seems to leap off the page at us and really "hits home" or leaves us with a warm glow inside. Have you ever had this happen and thought, "Ah, this morning I've met with God"? But the next few days as you read the Scripture nothing comparable happened, and you began to have that let-down feeling. We need to realize that a right evalua- of our quiet time has nothing to do with emotional responses, which change so easily. A right evaluation is based, instead, on our recognition of the fact that God, who never changes, has met with us.

### Prayer

The other vital part of our secret fellowship with God is prayer. It is just as necessary as Bible-reading if our inner lives are

1 *Search the Scriptures* ($4.50) is a single-volume guide that takes you through the entire Bible in three years. *This Morning with God* (in four volumes, $1.50 each) is an inductive approach that takes almost five years. Both are available from Inter-Varsity Press, Box F, Downers Grove, Illinois, 60515. Scripture Union provides a monthly graded series of studies for specific age groups (Write to Box 269, Upper Darby, Pa. 19082 for information about *Daily Bread* and other individual plans for family devotions.)

going to result in outward lives of spiritual power. We noted in passing that drawing from the Scriptures can freshen and vitalize a prayer life that's gone stale. Now we need to become more specific.

I'm sure we could all name the different aspects of prayer: worship, thanksgiving, confession, intercession for others, and petition for ourselves. But few of us even begin to give equal time to each aspect. Like me, you probably have gimme-itis: "Gimme, gimme, gimme! Lord, I need this, I just have to have that." And you probably tend to be weakest in worshipful praying. We seldom take time quietly, alone in His presence, to realize and acknowledge the worth-ship of God. To worship is to acknowledge the character of God Himself—not for what we can get out of either Him or our acknowledgment of Him but to acknowledge Him for Himself. We who aren't very good at worshiping can "prime the pump" by turning to some great hymn of the Church and making its words our own expression of worship. When I'm spiritually dry I often choose a psalm (like 103) or a hymn by one of the great saints of the past. For instance:

*Join all the glorious names of wisdom, love, and power,*
*That ever mortals knew, that angels ever bore*
*All are too mean to speak His worth,*
*Too mean to set my Savior forth.*

Or Bernard of Clairvaux's centuries-old expression:

*Jesus, Thou Joy of loving hearts,*
*Thou Fount of life, Thou Light of men,*
*From the best bliss that earth imparts*
*We turn unfilled to Thee again.*

As we share the spiritual experiences of these saints of the past, our own hearts well up in praise, adoration, and worship to the living God. Such worship brings us into the presence of God, lost in wonder, caught up in what Dr. Tozer called "the gaze of the soul."

## Establish Priorities

You can't worship like this in the last two minutes before dashing off to class. The major lack in our American "society of leisure" is time; we never seem to have enough. In the East the art of meditation has been widely cultivated, but even there modern technology is robbing people of their solitude. But everyone still has twenty-four hours in each day. And most of us have a measure of control over many of those hours. Usually we can find time for what we want, even if we have to take time from another activity. The most crucial battle in our lives is the continuing one of securing enough time alone in the presence of God. Our spiritual vigor and vitality in everything else depend on the outcome of this battle.

Just as the enemy of men's souls uses every possible means to sow secret sin in our lives, he will do everything in his power to prevent the development of a fruitful secret life with God. Innocent, innocuous things like assignments, a phone call, somebody wanting us to go to breakfast twenty minutes early constantly conspire to cut short or cut out our daily meeting with the living God.

One summer recently I had the privilege of hearing John Stott, the rector of one of the leading Anglican churches in London. He was speaking to ministers at the great Keswick Convention in the Lake District of England. His subject was priorities. The development of our inner lives, he pointed out, is the first priority for every Christian—including the minister. But he admitted a very strange paradox in his own life: "The thing I know will give me the deepest joy—namely, to be alone and unhurried in the presence of God, aware of His presence, my heart open to worship Him— is often the thing I least want to do." We are all victims of this paradox. The basic cause lies with our enemy, for he knows that we grow in spiritual power as we spend time with God. The devil will try anything, even misdirecting our desires, to attack the source of our spiritual power. There is profound truth in the little ditty, "Satan trembles when he sees the weakest Christian on his knees."

Some people claim that spending a set time with God every day is too routine, or too legalistic. Personal devotions can become legalistic or mechanical, but they don't need to. When they do, healthy discipline has been converted into bondage. Bondage suggests a thing we're forced to do, something that's an odious, hateful burden for us. Self-discipline applies to what we do voluntarily to avoid pain or secure a benefit. For spiritual growth through secret fellowship with God, we need positive discipline—now. As one who left the campus living situation some years ago, I can assure you that maintaining the secret life with God doesn't get any easier after you leave the campus. If you're going to set a pattern for life, now is the time to do it.

This essential disciplined regularity does not imply iron-clad rigidity. The stars won't fall out of heaven the day one of us has to skip his quiet time. We don't need to fear that everything will be lost, that we'll flunk our finals, that nothing will go right, etc, etc., just because we miss one day's quiet time. Not at all: God is not a tyrant who punishes us in such a way. However, He does expect us to take our spiritual life as seriously as we do our physical well-being. Our bodies need food, so we eat every day. Our spiritual lives need spiritual food; we should feed our souls with the Word of God every day. If we don't get the food we need, weakness soon sets in. We can't get by for long without food in either our physical or our spiritual life.

Although we're usually more concerned with the outward appearances, God's chief concern is with our inner life. He wants us to realize that all evidence of outward reality in our lives springs from the inner reality which only He can give us. He knows if secret sin is robbing us of spiritual power. He knows if we're reaping the full benefits of a secret life shared with Him.

The beginning of spiritual reality is total commitment to Jesus Christ evidenced by a desire to obey Him. The maintenance and development of spiritual vitality is through daily fellowship which results in a life of obedience and spiritual power.

Inner spiritual reality developed by a secret life with God is essential for an effective witness to a pagan world.

*It's what's inside that counts.*